An Exquisite Heritage

The Forager Rock Art of Zimbabwe

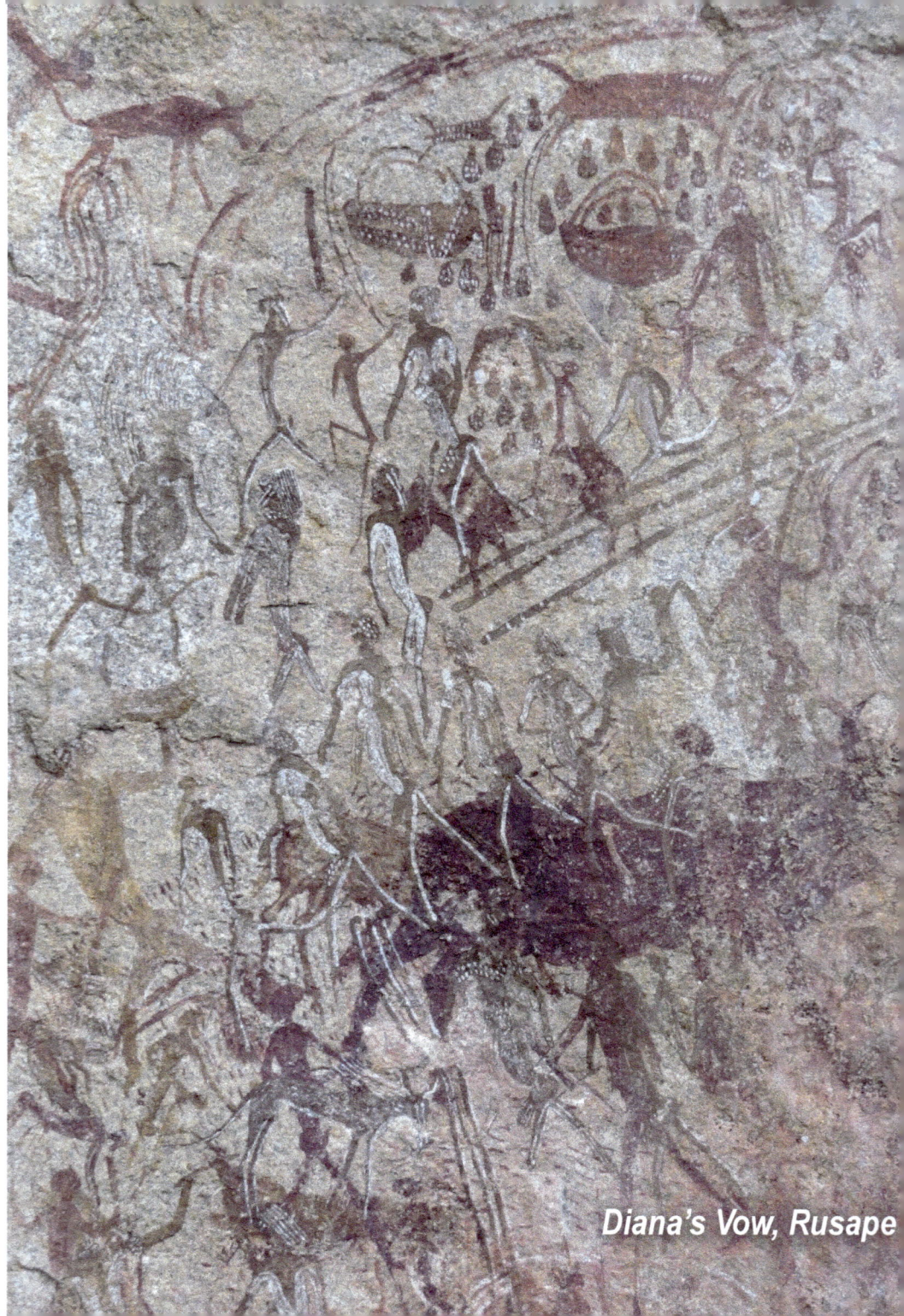
Diana's Vow, Rusape

An Exquisite Heritage

The Forager Rock Art of Zimbabwe

Rob Burrett and Russell Burrett-Feldman

2020

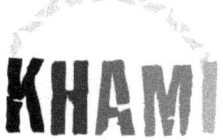

Copyright © 2020 by Rob Burrett, Khami Press

All rights reserved. This book or any portion thereof may not be reproduced or used in any manner whatsoever without the express written permission of the publisher except for the use of brief quotations in a book review or scholarly journal.

Revised Printing: 2020

ISBN 9-781716-494949

Khami Press
P.O. Box 27
Bulawayo, Zimbabwe

khamipress@gmail.com

Acknowledgements

The authors would like to thank friends and colleagues for reading the manuscript and/or offering valuable comments over the years as we pottered around in this complex field of rock art studies. In particular we must mention Stuart Beverley; Teresa Burrett; David Coulson; Stuart Danks; Janette Deacon; Julia Duprée; Adele Hamilton-Ritchie; Paul Hubbard; Ancila Nhamo; the late Elspeth Parry; Todini Runganga; Delores Smith; Gavin Stephens; Paul Stidolph; the late Sininisabo Tshuma; Kevin van Breda; Jonathan Waters; Paula Worsley-Worwick. Thanks also to Saint George's College, Harare for allowing me to photograph some of the unique artefacts in their collection, materials collected by several early Jesuit scholars. For all remaining errors and ambiguities in this booklet we must take responsibility.

Contents

What is Rock Art ? 1

Landscapes and Art 5

The Artists' Community 13

    Dating of the Art 17

    How was the Rock Art done? 20

The Human Image 25

    Bodily Form 26

    Material Culture and Hidden Meanings 34

    The Social Being 41

The Animal Symbol 57

Plants and the Cosmos 83

Abstract Images of Association 87

Zimbabwe's Exquisite Heritage 93

References 94

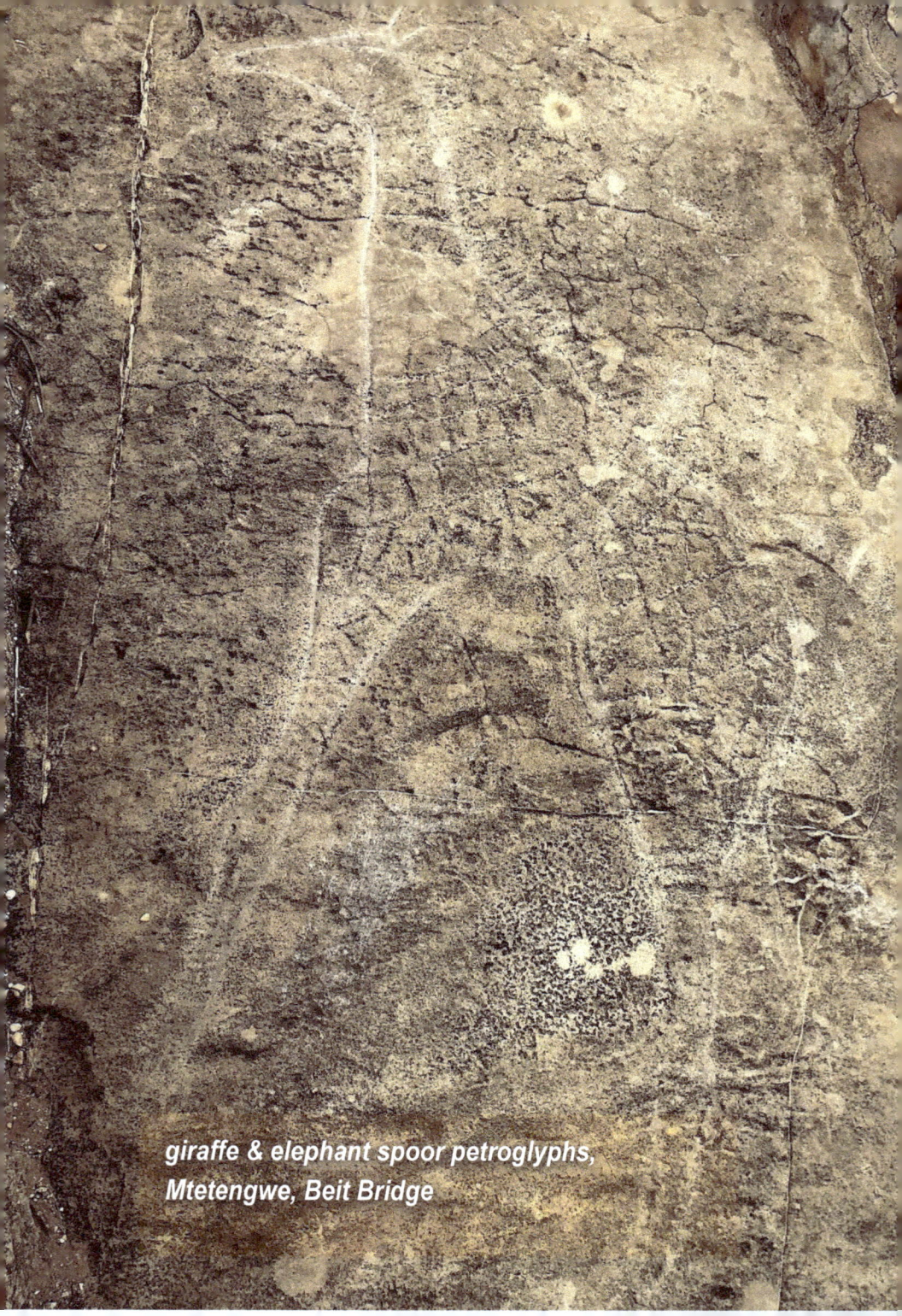

giraffe & elephant spoor petroglyphs, Mtetengwe, Beit Bridge

What is Rock Art ?

One of Zimbabwe's great, usually forgotten treasures is its unique rock art. Scattered across our country, we have one of the world's most extensive collections of prehistoric rock art. This is a valuable cultural heritage that has been left to us by our distant ancestors and it deserves to be better appreciated.

Most of the art is painted, although in places there are engravings where images were carved or scratched into relatively soft rock. These engravings, sometimes called *petroglyphs*, are limited to the Karoo Sandstone exposures of the Hwange District and the Save and Limpopo Valleys, as well as the weathered dolerites at several isolated locations of the Eastern Highlands.

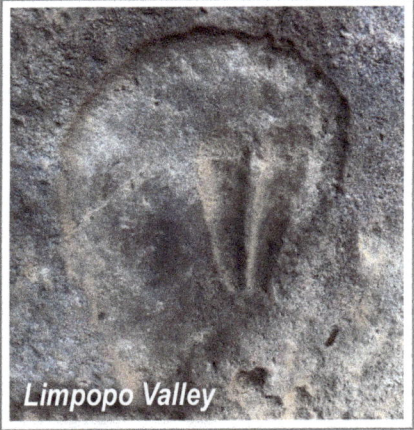
Limpopo Valley

This booklet provides an introduction, a personal reflection, to this rich visual heritage. It tackles some of the many questions we are often asked, as well as interrogating the unsaid preconceptions that often cloud our understanding and explanation of the art.

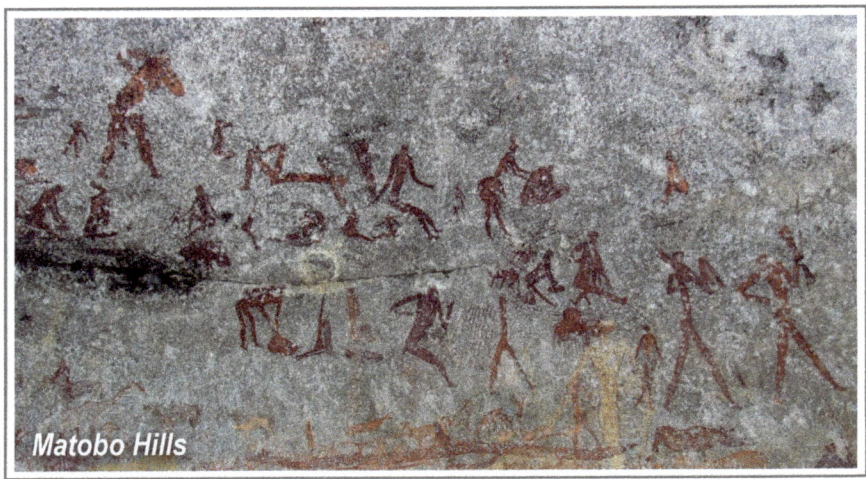
Matobo Hills

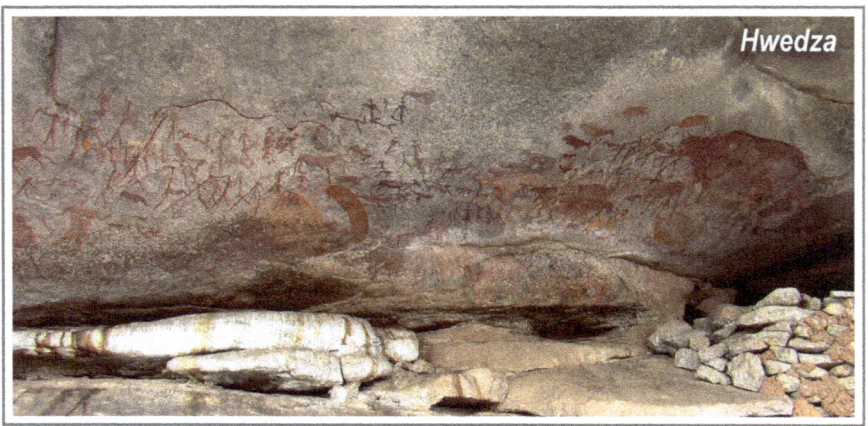
Hwedza

There are literally thousands of rock art sites scattered across the country, ranging from large caves to isolated images painted on scattered boulders. Some authors have suggested that there are anything between 10,000 to 30,000 painted sites. we believe that it is somewhere in the upper range of these figures, or even many more. No one can hope to cover all of them.

At the onset we must divest ourselves of the preconception that the art was straightforward; mere random images created by idle minds or some form of ancient *interior decorating.* Nor were they simple journalistic narratives. The art is in fact a portrayal of select polysemantic[1] symbols which bear witness to past human beliefs and ways of life. They were a means of visual communication by which the long lost artists tried to rationalise the complex natural and social contexts. Making use of their own culturally-defined knowledge of the world around them, the images they painted or engraved were selective in what was and, as equally important, what was not shown, as well as through the associations of symbols created by juxtaposition and superimposition[2]. The art was a cultural language which, through a visual medium, dealt with the complexities of human experience, hopes, aspirations and the cosmological philosophy of the now lost or acculturated communities that once created it.

---

1 Polysemantic = having many meanings, some of which are somewhat ambiguous

2 Juxtaposition = intentionally painted alongside another image to create a meaningful combination; superimposition = painted on top of another to create a meaningful combination of symbolism.

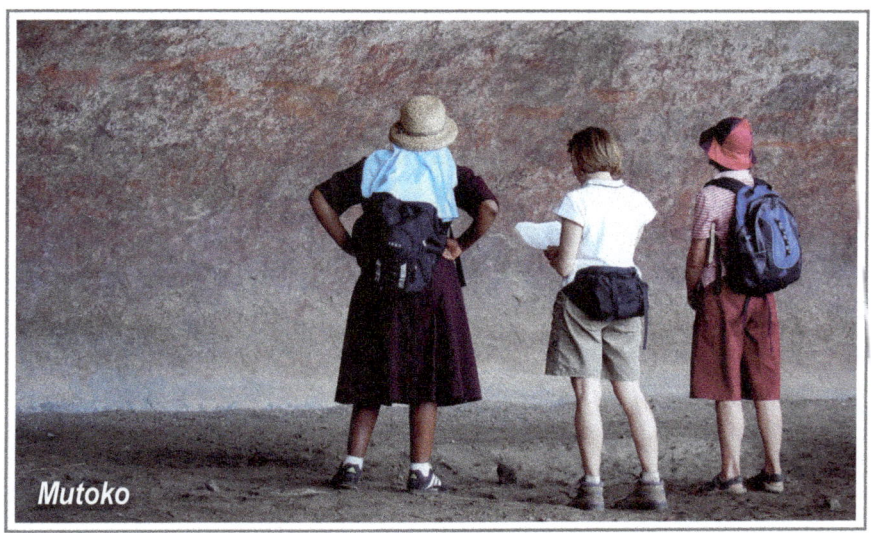
Mutoko

To truly appreciate our rock art, we must understand that it was part of a socially-constructed world quite unlike our own. All too often we read or hear superficial interpretations; explanations determined by the modern socio-cultural perceptions and symbolism of the author, tour guide or academic school of thought. It is wrong to impose our own contemporary individual and social concerns onto the worldly experiences of old. We argue that we must first endeavour to liberate ourselves from our own cultural baggage, and attempt to see art through the eyes of the artist creator.

Let it be understood that this is not simply a Eurocentric challenge or failing. All groups bring with them their own cultural perceptions which redefine the art into the symbolic experiences of their own background. We have heard and seen the art equally reinterpreted by many Shona and Ndebele traditionalists who feel they too can declare the *obvious*, paying little heed to the cultures of another community.

While it is true that the artists' way of life and their symbolic codes no longer exist, through careful reference to ethnographic material we believe that we can achieve at least a partial grasp of what was once being said. Yes, we will never have a full understanding as too many pages of the story have been torn out of the book of human history, but we can (and should) learn to appreciate the art through the eyes of the artists' own society.

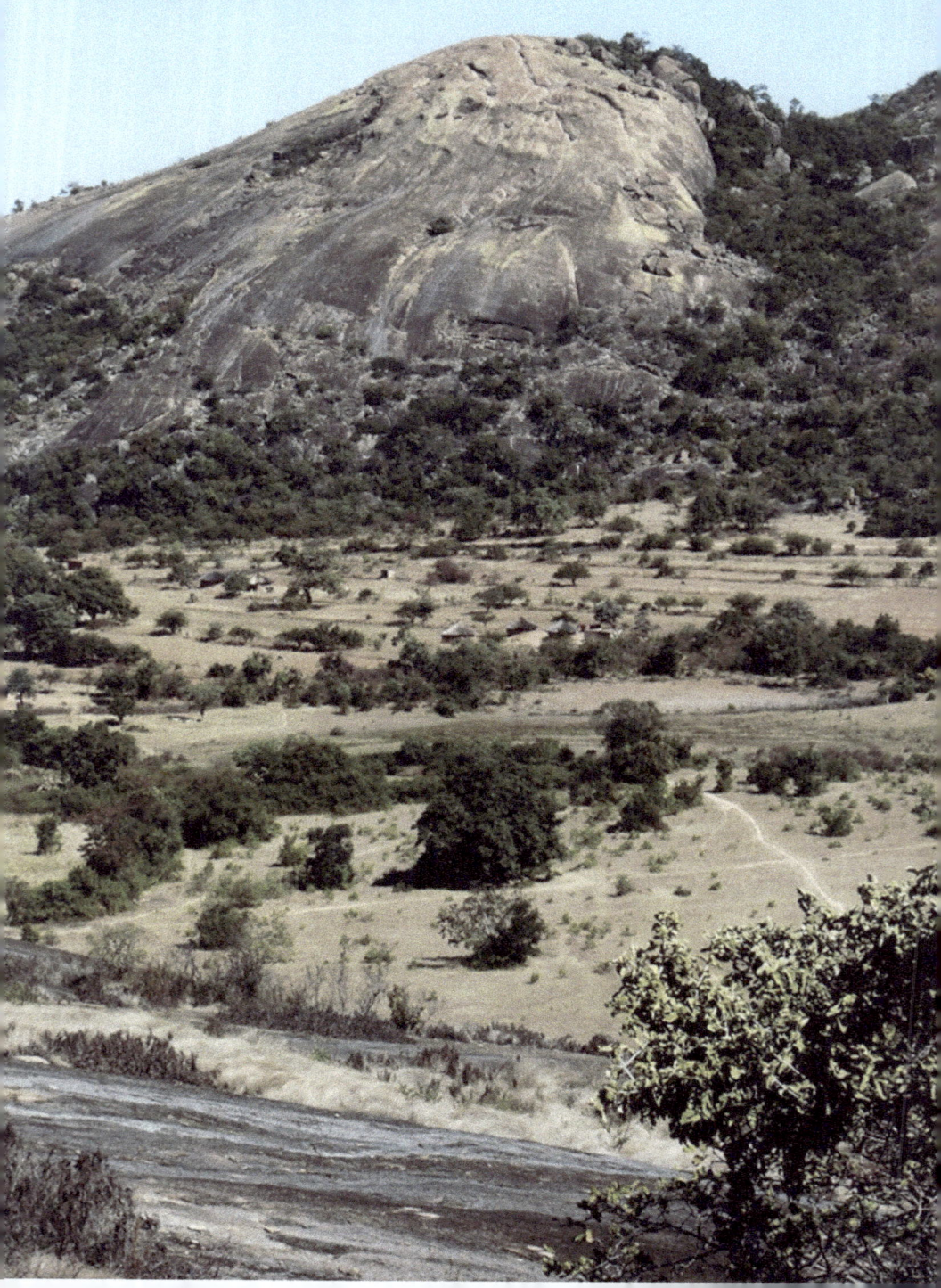
The Eastern Matobo Hills

Landscapes and Art

The granite outcrops of central Zimbabwe are particularly rich in painted sites. Here numerous shallow caves and rocky overhangs provided the artists with many a suitable canvas. In other places, they painted on the sides of isolated boulders where the images are exposed to the elements and most have been lost to us. It was through the creation of the art that the artists and their communities actively transformed a natural geomorphological terrain into a fascinating human, spiritual landscape.

Zimbabwe's ancient granites originated as molten masses of liquid rock which cooled deep below the earth's surface some time between 3,000 and 2,000 million years ago. It intruded into and distorted older rocks, the Greenstone Belts. These were often the source of the pigments used in the art, but rarely do they provide suitable rock faces for painting or engraving.

After formation, the subterranean granite was steadily exposed as the overlying rocks were eroded. Infinitesimally slow in the sense of human history, this erosion has left behind harder outcrops of unweathered granite. These form characteristic hills or inselbergs - bornhardts/whalebacks/*dwala* are massive, dome-like swellings of solid rock; and tors/castle kopjes/*amaqaqa* are localised accumulations of smaller,

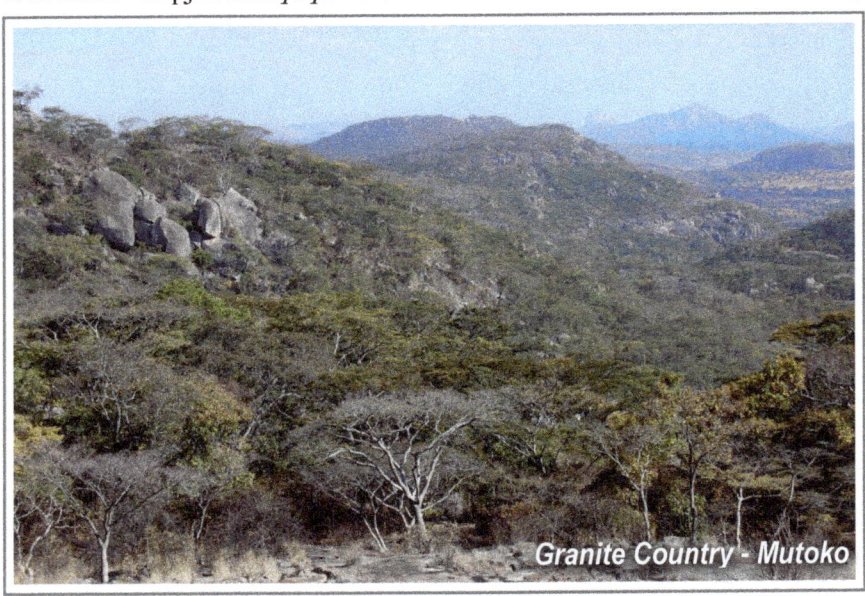
Granite Country - Mutoko

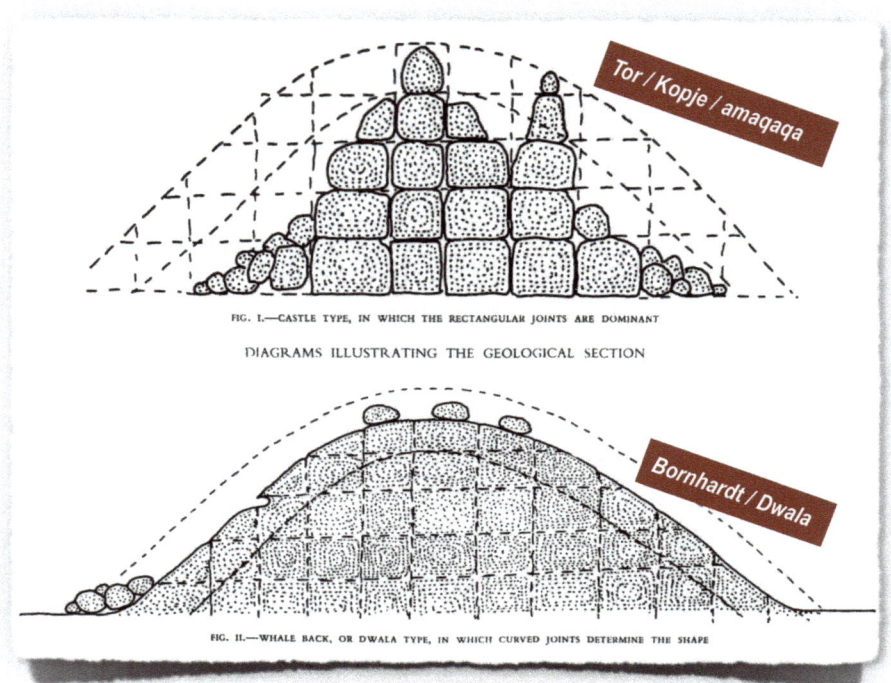

FIG. I.—CASTLE TYPE, IN WHICH THE RECTANGULAR JOINTS ARE DOMINANT

DIAGRAMS ILLUSTRATING THE GEOLOGICAL SECTION

FIG. II.—WHALE BACK, OR DWALA TYPE, IN WHICH CURVED JOINTS DETERMINE THE SHAPE

(After Tredgold, 1956:34)

weathered blocks of granite which have been left balancing upon each other. Both of these landscape forms, and many intermediate combinations, are the result of subsurface chemical weathering along different patterns of rock cracks (joints) prior to erosion. Once exposed, surface weathering has maintained the shapes of these rocky hills through gradual exfoliation and chemical decay. These are landscapes of a remarkable age, many thousands of years old.

In some places natural caves and rock shelters have formed as a result of subsurface chemical weathering along prominent lines of weakness in the granite. These joints, along which concave chemical etching was initiated, can often be seen in the rear walls of caves where they are marked as small crevices and holes, easily perceived as hollows into the spiritual world within. Following surface exposure, these inverse dome-like hollows are subject to gradual negative spheroidal weathering (exfoliation in reverse). Being shaded, moister areas the granite walls of these shelters are subject to enhanced biological activity, and thin spalls

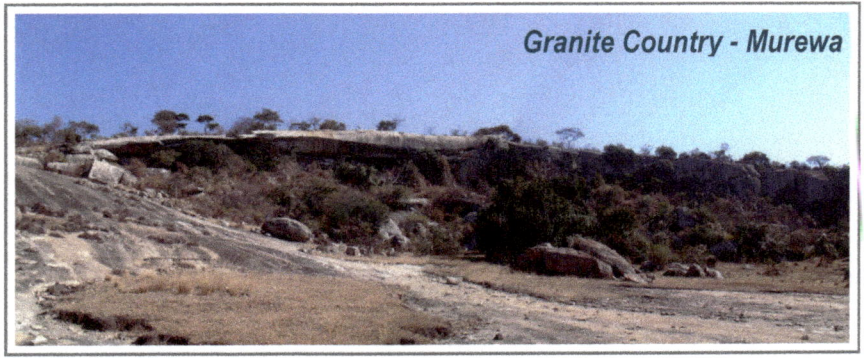

of rock gradually peal away so expanding the caves backward. This is an entirely natural process that will eventually destroy the painted canvas, so depriving us of the art. Unfortunately, adverse human activity can speed up this rate of destruction.

Rock art is found throughout most of Zimbabwe's broken granite landscapes, although there are several particularly noteworthy concentrations. These were probably special spiritual places, locations to which people gravitated in times of social and economic stress, as well as being centres selected for periodic ceremonies. This may account for the remarkable concentration and diversity of art to be found in the Mutoko and Murewa Districts; the Matobo Hills near Bulawayo; the granite hills which lie between Harare and Bindura; the northwestern foothills of the Nyanga Highlands; and the Zaka District of Masvingo.

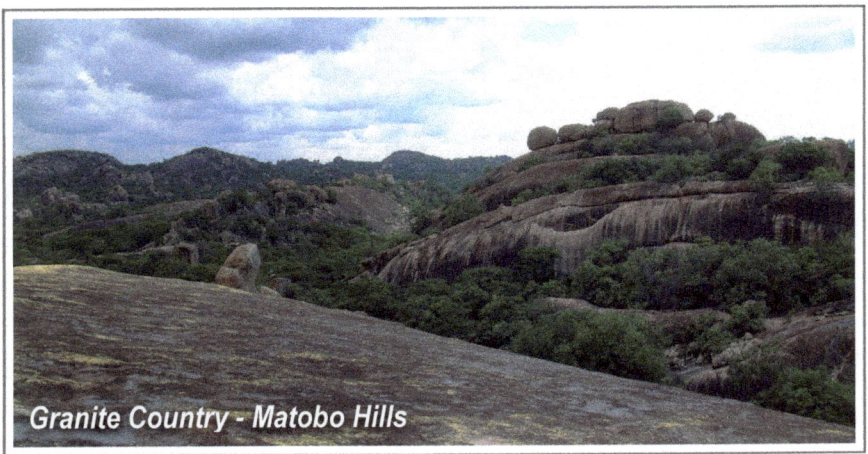

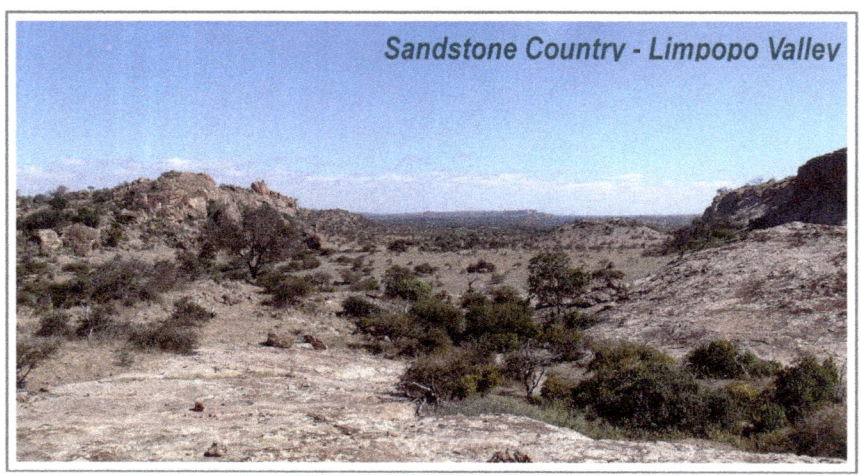

Sandstone Country - Limpopo Valley

In those areas of Karoo Sediments, rocks a mere 280 - 210 million years old, gradual surface decay along lines of weakness in the sandstone has, in some places, resulted in shallow, linear caves which were often painted in the past. Elsewhere, shallow hollows form below fallen boulders, the result of a localised combination of shade, moisture and biological activity. In the sandstone hills around Chiredzi, in the Limpopo River Valley near Beit Bridge, and in the Hwange District, we find distinct traditions of paintings and/or rock engravings.

Each of these regional centres of art have distinct local styles and symbolic content. We recommend visiting as many of them as possible

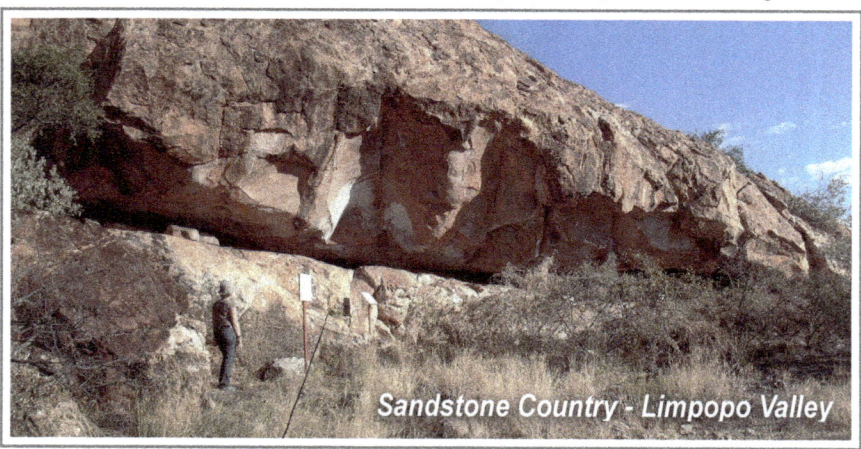

Sandstone Country - Limpopo Valley

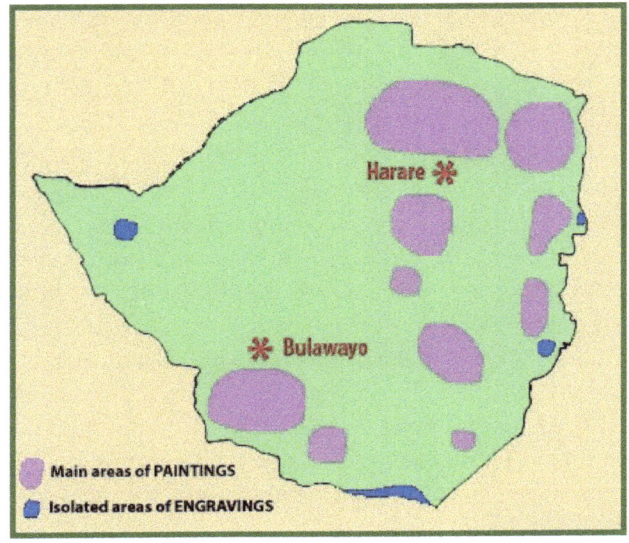

should you wish to get a fuller understanding of our diverse artistic heritage.

On the whole most other Zimbabwean rock types were unsuitable as far as prehistoric art. They were rarely painted or engraved given the absence of natural shelters, or natural canvas was too dark/rough/fragile/soft to attract the efforts of the artists. The sedimentary and metamorphic rocks of northeastern Zimbabwe have little in the way of rock art, although near Chinhoyi several painted panels are known in small shelters which have formed in the crystalline dolomite. Similarly, the deeply-weathered, gneissic plains in the central part of the country and the sandy expanses of the Kalahari Sands in the west are devoid of rock art. In particular, isolated paintings can be found in remote corners of the rugged Chimanimani Mountains. Possibly this was one of the final social refuges for Forager artists in historical times.

These ancient landscapes are more than a neutral geomorphological setting for the art; they are a unique artistic gallery in which the very echoes of past human cosmology and ritual have become inscribed. Resonance of the past has transformed these rocky landscapes into sacred places, creating spiritual landscapes which call out to sapient emotion, now as much as they did in the past.

It is certain that the Forager artists knew and appreciated every nook-and-cranny of their landscape. This was the socially-constructed terrain in which they lived; their territories or *n!oresi*[3] which provided

---

[3] A Ju/'hoan term - an existing Khoe-Sān community who still live in territories on the Botswana-Namibian border.

them with both living sustenance and a spiritual context wherein human life took place. Not all places would have been considered equal, some were singled out and used for specific purposes. Unfortunately, most of us tend to presume that all rock art sites, all places, were equal, the locations of habitation where people periodically lived and worked. This scenario is as unlikely in the past as it is now. Like us today, the artists compartmentalised their landscape, associating some places with specific economic and social activities. Select spaces would have been set aside for specific spiritual activities, such as various rites of passage, or specific economic activities undertaken at different times in the year. A consequence of this is that the repertoire of artistic symbols used, and the visual associations so made, will vary between contemporary sites. Add to this spatial variation, the complication of temporal changes in site access and the evolution of social norms, and it becomes clear that any interpretation of the rock art is no simple matter.

Most of the rock art images used in this booklet come from the larger, painted sites. They are most regularly visited because of their artistic diversity - they are the biggest and the best. Undoubtedly the visitor will be captivated by what can be seen, but it must be remembered that these are only some of Zimbabwe's many rock art sites. These bigger sites represent, we argue, centralised ceremonial centres wherein only part of the complicated symbolic code of the past was expressed. Our gut feeling is that the art in these centres was more standardised, the result of greater social conservatism which would have prevailed. In contrast, smaller rock shelters and isolated boulder images often exhibit a far greater range of artistic expression. We have here the assertion of the individual; a more everyday use and portrayal of the general artistic code that regulated the society. Here you will find a more diverse symbolic expression reflecting seasonally different socio-economic activities, demographics, age and gendered definitions. Many, if not most, of these smaller painted sites have as yet to be recorded by professionals and they are known only to those who live nearby. Yet, if you really want to understand Zimbabwe's rock art, it is important to visit such sites, going beyond the main tourist caves. We leave this exciting task up to you.

Before moving on to the social meaning and reasons for the art, perhaps it is appropriate here that we touch on the nature and social meaning of the very rock face on which we find the art. There was no physical preparation of the painted surface, these are natural rock faces protected from the elements, running water and intense biological-chemical decay. Nature alone provided what the artists required. Sadly, as local conditions change, as vegetation is removed or water trickles differently down the rock face, so the geological canvas degenerates and the art is destroyed and spirituality of the very landscape is lost forever. Please don't touch the art with fingers or pointers, limit the use of intense camera flashes, and NEVER wet the images to 'get a better view'. All of this will contribute to its decay and loss faster than necessary. However, do look and appreciate the art, for we are privileged in what we can still see.

It is probable that for the artists the painted rock faces were no mere natural surfaces, no neutral canvases. Some academics have described the rock face as a *sacred veil*, a curtain which separated the physical human world on the outside from the inner spiritual one obscured within the rock itself. With the painting of images of cosmological power, we see the coming together of the people and the spirits. The acts of painting and contemplation, and maybe even prehistoric touching of the rock face, fused these worlds together. This merging of life and hidden spirituality often focuses on natural cracks and hollows in the rock face - portals to the beyond. Human and animal figures, as well as lines and abstract forms, appear to merge into or come out of these natural disjunctures in the rock face, so expressing the artists' belief of spirituality moving in both directions. At the well known cave of Nswatugi in the Matobo Hills, illustrated here, the mass of painted images appear to emanate and spread forth from the natural hollows at the rear of the cave; all life appears to emerge from within the rock.

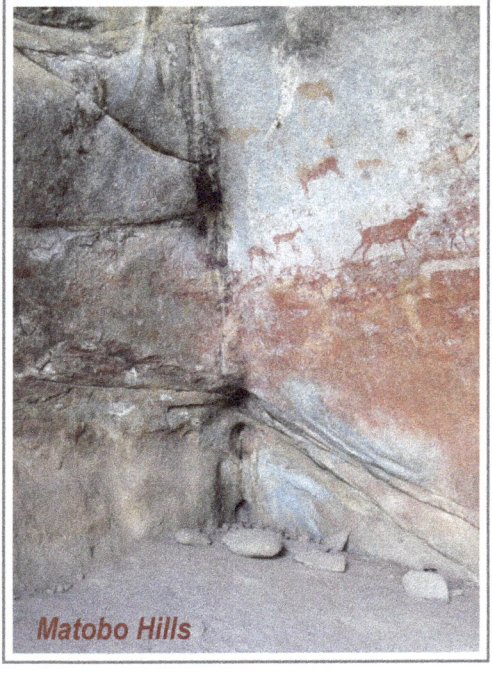
Matobo Hills

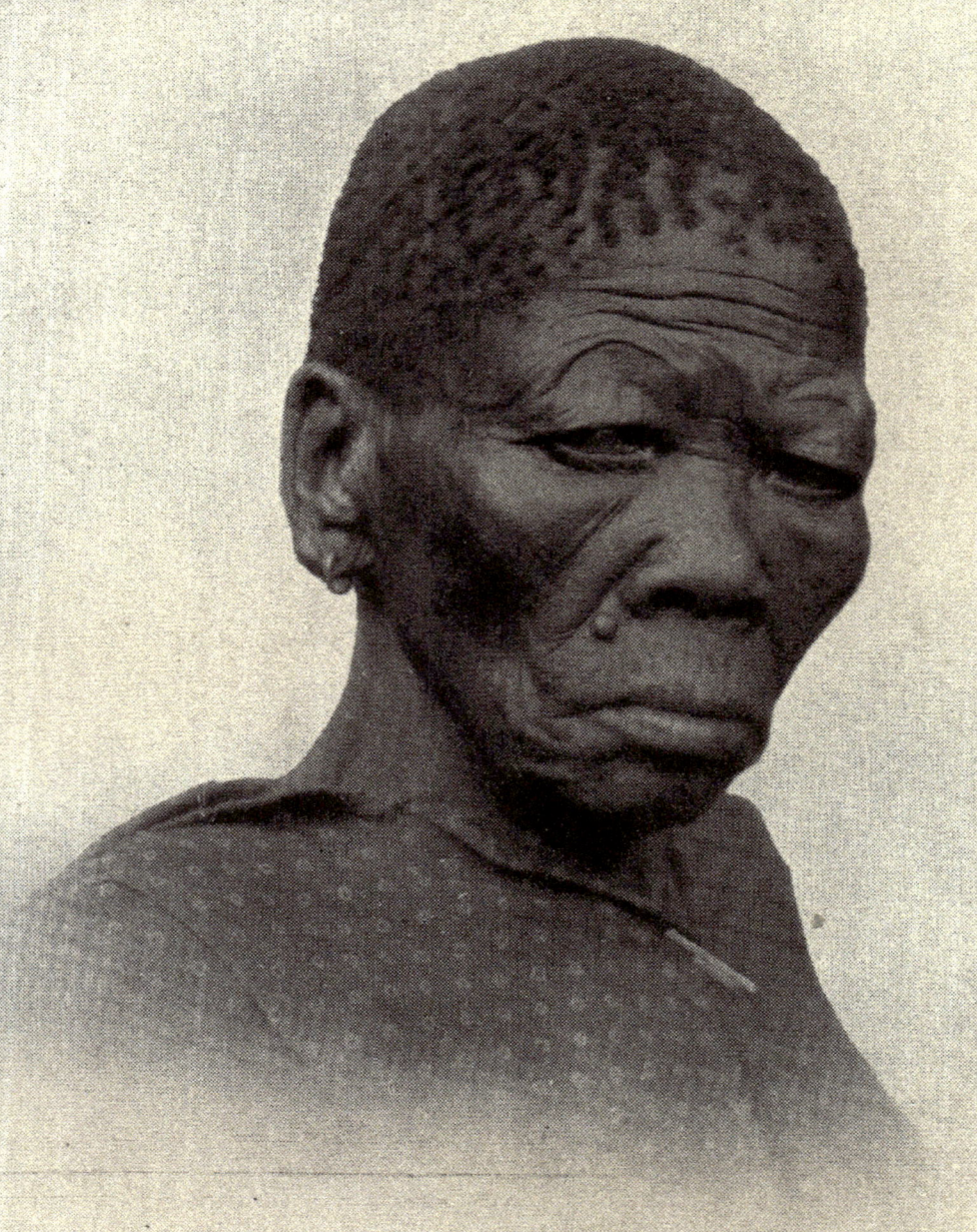

Bamtshayile
Enyandeni, Matobo Hills, Circa 1920
(After Jones, 1926:63-65)

The Artists' Community

Most of Zimbabwe's rock art was created by hunter-gatherers (foragers), a community which once lived off the rich bounty of the countryside. They collected wild plants and small animals, and hunted larger prey, mostly the antelope, that were once common throughout the land. Nature provided everything that they needed - their food, tools, medicines and even their religious symbols. In this booklet, we focus on these forager artists. Some reference will, however, also be made to the later agriculturalist and pastoralist rock art. Far less common in Zimbabwe, their art is a study seriously in need of academic investigation. Likewise, our emphasis is on the painted art as the engraved depictions have been equally overlooked.

It must be understood at the onset that the art is not the work of some foreign migrants. Rather, it was painted or engraved by the distant forager ancestors of Zimbabwe's indigenous people. They were members of the Sān-related peoples who once dominated Southern Africa, a subcontinental regional evolutionary diversification of humanity. We avoid the use of the term *Bushmen* as the name has unwanted racial connotations, being a derogatory dismissal of the local inhabitants by later migrant communities. Admittedly, the alternative term Sān is itself not without complication. It represents twentieth century academic nomenclature and its use in the literature has resulted in further unwanted implications regarding perceived ownership and the preservation of our artistic heritage[4]. It reinforces the notion that the art is the product of some OTHER community, one entirely distinct from the current black majority Africans. This may be so to some degree as far as economic and social systems are concerned, but it is factually incorrect when it comes to basic genetics.

After centuries of social transformation and intermarriage with other African migrants who increasingly arrived in the last two millennia, most indigenous Zimbabweans are related in some way to these distant

---

[4] The word Sān was originally Khoe, the historical pastoralist communities of southern Africa,. They considered themselves culturally and economically superiority over the Sān, their word for the foragers whom they regarded as outsiders, the people of the wilds. Unfortunately, the word Sān has many similar racial overtones to the European epithet, "bushmen". Yet today, there are many who now use the word Sān for themselves as a distinct community of "First Peoples", proud of a foraging ancestry. Naming can be be a complicated matter, imbued with social and political undertones, in the past as much as in the present.

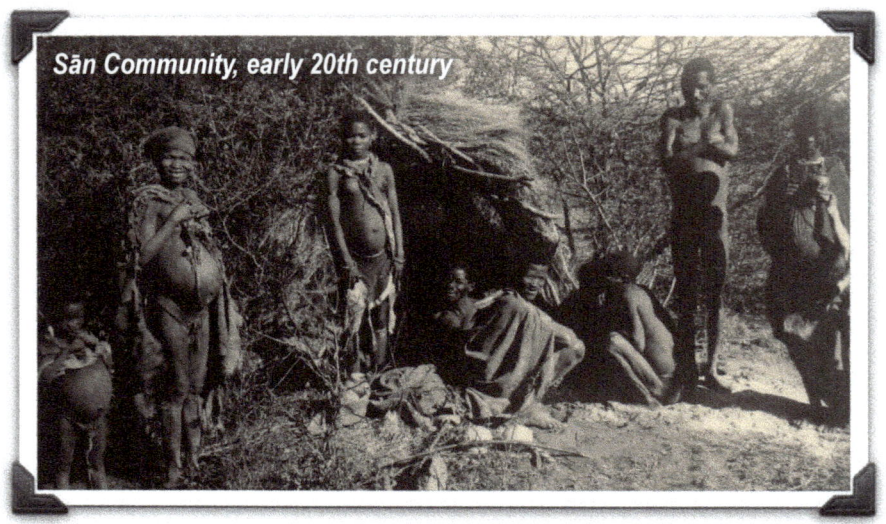
Sān Community, early 20th century

ancestors. These later migrants brought with them a new way of life sustained by animal rearing and farming, and in the face of these changes the existing forager communities responded. Some separated themselves entirely, seeking to preserve their way of life in isolation. However, many more took advantage of the new social and economic opportunities offered. The colonial image of cruel Bantu subjugation and alienation of the "innocent" and, of late, overtly romanticised *bushmen* has been exaggerated; a story used by other newcomers to justify a particular version of history. It fails to recognise the very fluid nature of humanity's changing allegiances and creating and re-creating of personal and community identities. Unfortunately this segregationist perception of *an other*, that is groups not my own, prevails in many Zimbabwean minds. It is a colonisation of perception. As a result, many indigenous Zimbabweans consider the art as foreign, a product not of their own blood. They take little care in its preservation, and some groups even go so far as to intentionally destroy it.

    The bulk, but not all, of our rock art is of forager origin. In southern Zimbabwe Khoe pastoralists are believed to have been responsible for some of the schematic depictions in the Limpopo Valley and possibly also in the Matobo Hills. Since the mid eighteenth century, small groups of Northern Sotho, Venda and Nguni migrants migrated into southwestern Zimbabwe from what is today South Africa. They brought with them a distinct tradition of symbols painted during initiation ceremonies. Often

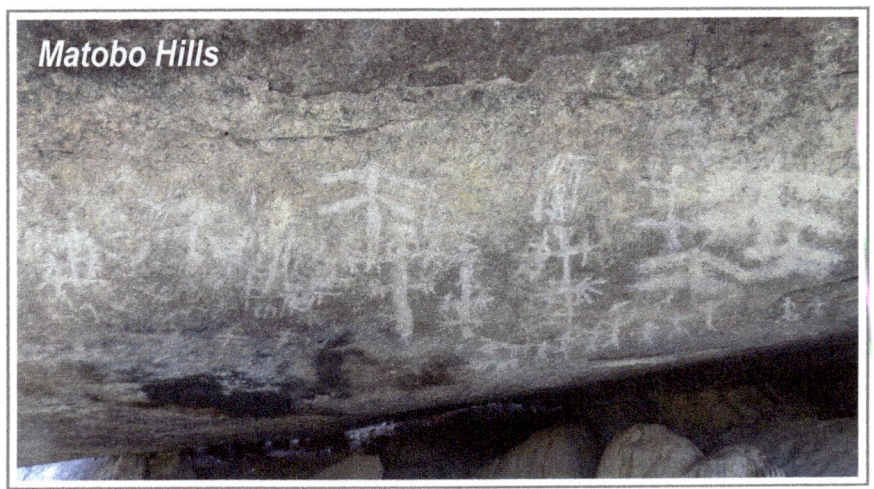

covering the earlier hunter-gatherer depictions, these groups intentionally reused older forager-painted sites seeking to capture the religious resonance of such places. Later still, twentieth century migrants from Zambia, Malawi and Tanzania brought with them to many areas, particularly Mashonaland, their own artistic traditions. They too often reused existing painted sites as part of the activities associated with their sacred ceremonial cults.

Sadly, the locations and meanings of these later depictions, often dismissed as crude copies or vandalism, have not received the academic attention that they deserve. The so-called *late whites* (although some are in red) are sometimes mentioned in reports, but are generally ignored. In so doing, we miss out on a whole layer of use of space, spirituality and social action. We hope that current research will soon rectify this situation.

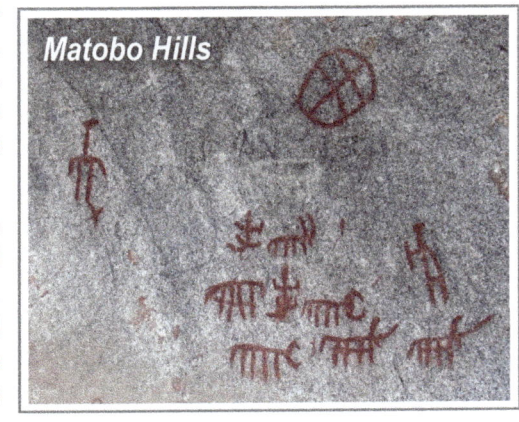

Then there is the modern graffiti, often found scrawled over the older forager art. Sometimes we find ourselves questioning the very nature and motives

15

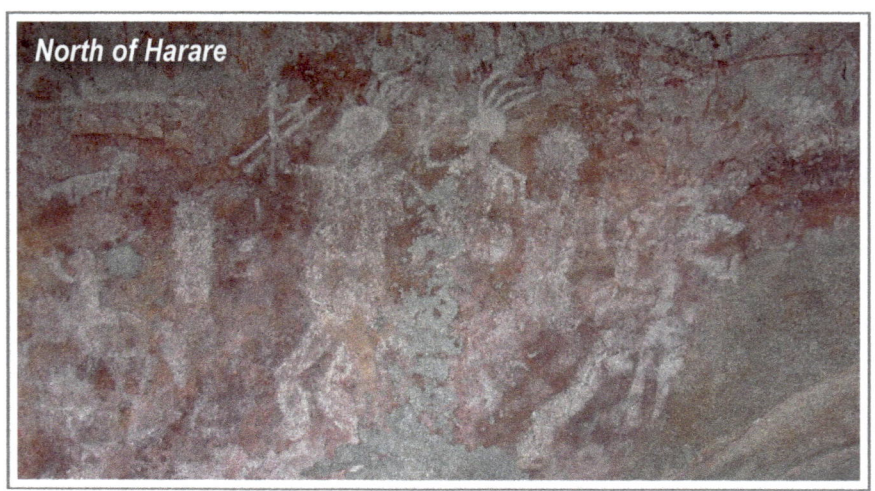

North of Harare

behind this. It too is a social product; a statement of individual and community perceptions of the older art, and reusing of the sacred space.

Some may object to our apparent liberalism in not condemning it outright. Yes, we are offended by it, but we believe that it is important to try and understand why people today seek to make their mark, destroying the past. Is the graffiti ignorance that such acts obliterate an integral part of their ancestry? Or is it a statement of modern politics, an act of anti-establishment on the part of a disenchanted Zimbabwean youth? Or is it an economic backlash where local people see *rich* visitors fawning over rock art in their backyards, all the while those who live with it are mired in poverty? It is too simplistic to jump up and down and decry you bad people. Ultimately, the preservation of our art requires more than emotive knee-jerk reactions.

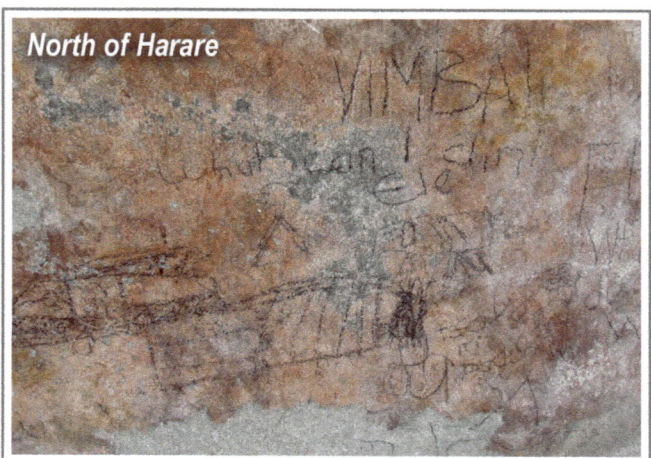

North of Harare

Dating of the Art

The matter of age is a complicated one. Excluding modern graffiti, the art of migrant farming communities may be as recent as the colonial era, although it is unlikely that it is still being painted today. In Zimbabwe, there is also no tradition of actively repainting as can be found in some communities in Australia, ours is indeed a lost tradition of some antiquity.

The precise age of the earlier forager art remains uncertain. Until recently there was no means of direct dating of the images, as standard archaeological techniques require the recovery of uncontaminated organic material. Unfortunately, this is not present, as most images are now little more than an ochre stain or weathered engraving. In the absence of science, most authors and guides have resorted to sweeping generalisations associating the art with the Later Stone Age, an archaeological entity linked to the ancestors of the historical Sān communities of the region. This suggests that the art dates to anything between 30,000 to 2,000 years ago. While there is some truth in this, it rests on three unproven assumptions - that the to the Later Stone Age; that it was a tradition wholly limited to the Sān; and that the advent of farming resulted in the rapid disappearance of all hunter-gatherers about the start of the Christian era.

Is is worth reconsidering these assumptions. There is no reason that the art is all Sān, all hunter-gatherer, or all Later Stone Age. Indeed, recent discoveries at several caves in South Africa have extended back the history of art into the more remote past, into the so-called Middle Stone Age. It may be associated with the emergence of modern humans, the Southern African regional evolution of the Sān genetic cluster, around 115,000 years ago. A spectacular discovery was made at Blombos Cave in the southern Cape where an engraved block of ochre, an engraved bone fragment, and ochre-painted rock flakes date to sometime between 70,000 to 100,000 years before present. Clearly humanity's artistic desire has a much greater time depth than has previously been thought. We *modern people* tend to look down on these distant ancestors as being incapable of the cognitive capacity which we believe defines us as a superior thinking species. Yet art was indeed there, although the passage of time and exposure to the elements has all but destroyed most of what was once there.

Excavations at Apollo 11 Shelter in southern Namibia have yielded several painted stones which are firmly dated to 30,000 years old. In

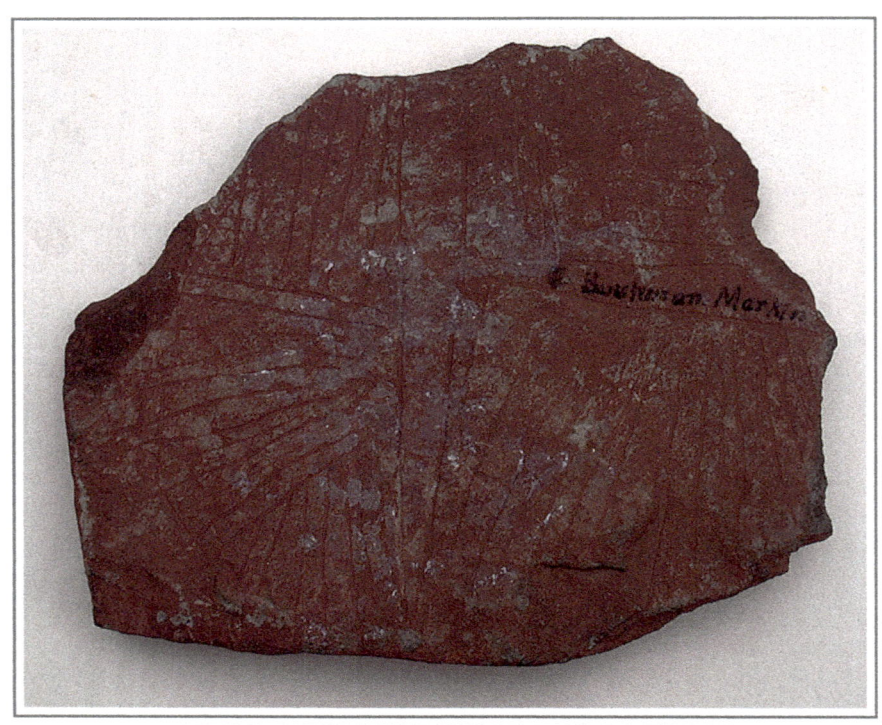

Engraved Stone, unknown location, Matobo Hills

Zimbabwe, excavations at Pomongwe Cave in the Matobo Hills south of Bulawayo, yielded four painted rock spalls, slithers of granite exfoliated from the rock walls. These have been dated to at least 13,000 years before present. At the nearby Bambata Cave, an engraved stone with an incised grid-like pattern came from soft, ashy deposits which date to at least 8,500 years ago. These valuable fragments provide us with but a minimum date for our rock art. The cave walls were first painted and only later, after some unknown time interval, did the spalls flake off to become buried in the sediments on the cave floors.

Recently, a professional French research team, working with National Museums & Monuments of Zimbabwe and the University of Zimbabwe, used new techniques in an attempt to date some of the paintings in the Matobo Hills. Their work, still at a preliminary stage, suggests that some of the depictions are ancient, maybe as old as 14,000 years. These are exciting times and hopefully, should their efforts prove a success, we will

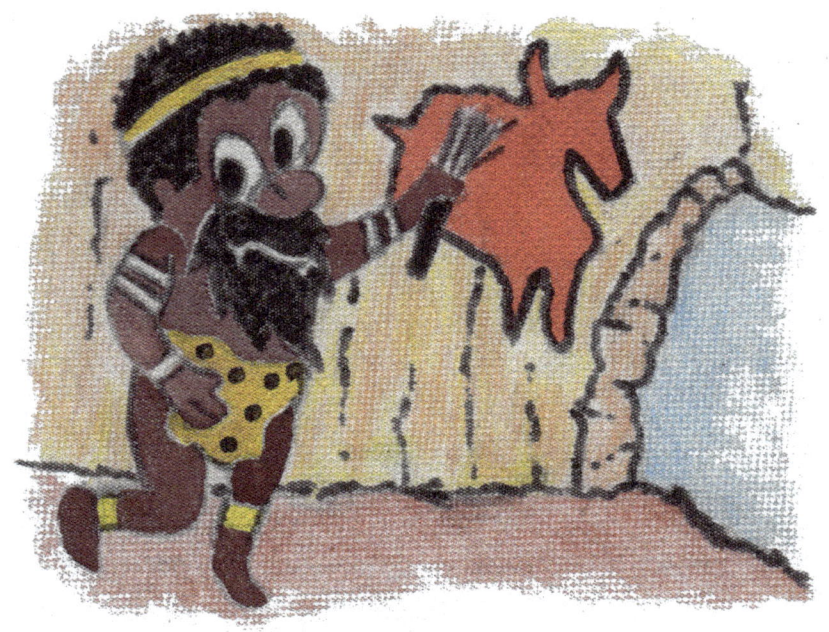

The "Sān Artist". A cartoon by the the late Sininisabo Tshuma for a booklet we did on the rock art for Zimbabwean primary schools in 2018. RIP our friend.

soon achieve a better chronological understanding of the art. We may be able to understand the complex temporal changes in both artistic style and symbolism. Previous attempts to define a chronology have been based on unwarranted assumptions as to the use of colour and painting techniques, and the results have proven idiosyncratic and hard to replicate. This new work, based on independent scientific techniques, may finally allow us to go forward.

It is always the archaeologist's ambition to find the oldest of everything, but what of the other end of the time scale? We believe that most of the surviving rock art which we see today is not as old as many suggest. Much of it probably dates to somewhere between 500 to 3,000 to 4,000 years before present. Most of the older depictions have already vanished, destroyed by biological activity, wind, rain and the sun. Only in a few protected places are traces of these older paintings likely to have been preserved, places like the deep caves of Mucheka in the Murewa District, or Pomongwe and Nanke Caves in the Matobo Hills.

It is equally unlikely that the forager artistic tradition stopped abruptly with the first arrival of farming about 2,000 years ago. Indeed, the social pressures generated by the presence of multiple communities with competing socio-economic systems may, in fact, have intensified the need for the artistic tradition as people sought solace in their own community identities and ceremonies. Yes, some areas and the larger caves may have been abandoned by the foragers, but archaeological evidence suggests that many of the smaller painted shelters were still inhabited, and presumably painted, in this more recent era of forager-farming contact. Increasingly the Sān eked out a living on the social and spatial margins of the farming majority. These last foraging peoples co-existed as a downtrodden class, economically linked to those who wielded power. We believe that, in these circumstances, the remaining foragers probably intensified their own traditions as a way of coping with their lot. There was a final, desperate expression of separate forager identity through rock art, rain-making and trance-related spiritual healing. Ultimately, history was against them and they were absorbed into the more dominant farming economy and social system.

How was the Rock Art done?

The paints used by the artists were derived from natural products picked up from the countryside and transformed in what was probably a ritualised process, heavy with symbolic associations. The paint itself became sacred, strengthened with spiritual power to transform human and natural events.

From nature, select clays and weathered rock residue (soft material known as ochre) were collected along the margins of the granite wetlands (vleis) or in the Greenstone Belts. This was then crushed to make a powder. Sometimes it was heated over a fire, changing the natural red ochre to brown, yellow or black powder dependent on the degree of oxidation induced by the heating process. Once the desired colour was achieved, the powder was mixed with a binding medium. We are not quite sure what this was. Experiments have shown that water alone does not work. The medium may have been animal fat, egg white, congealed blood, plant sap or a mixture. In the literature, several plant-based possibilities have been suggested, most especially powdered Acacia or *Commiphera* gum, or the sticky latex of *Euphorbia* species. This medium ensured that the mineral paint stuck to the rock face. In most cases, this original organic component has long since decayed, and all we are left with is an ochre stain on the rock face.

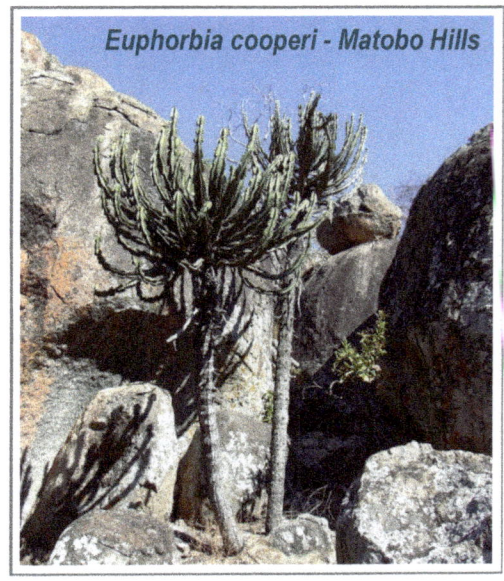

Euphorbia cooperi - Matobo Hills

It is likely that the artists first drew an outline on the rock, possibly with charcoal, then filled in the shape using a thin bone or wooden spatula, or paint brushes made from animal hair or masticated sticks. Where large areas had to be filled, the artists appear to have used their fingers. With the basic profile complete, finer details were added - ears, tails, the patches/stripes on the skins of many of the wild animals, hair, clothing and the implements held and ornaments worn by the people. Where the paintings are well preserved, it is evident that the artists spent a considerable amount of time, sometimes using different colours, to complete their work.

Many of these details were done in white paint, sometimes different shades of red. Manufactured from white clay or heated zinc/lead oxides, the white paint has, sadly, proven short-lived. It decays and fades quickly and as a consequence we have lost most of what was once depicted. In some of the larger caves you may, however, be lucky to find these details are preserved. Take a careful close-up look at the images, especially the smaller human figures. Occasionally all-white figures can be found, although they are often hard to make out without your nose almost on the rock face. It is probable that there were once many more such images, now lost to us.

In a few instances, the depictions were done as fine lines without shading. Never common, most images are of animals, especially (and

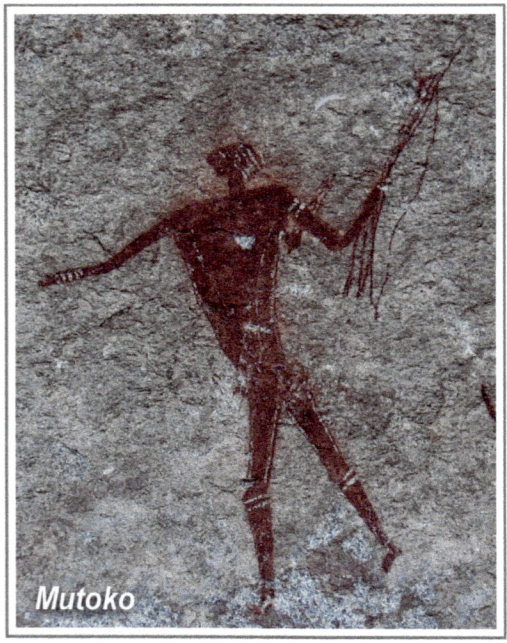
Mutoko

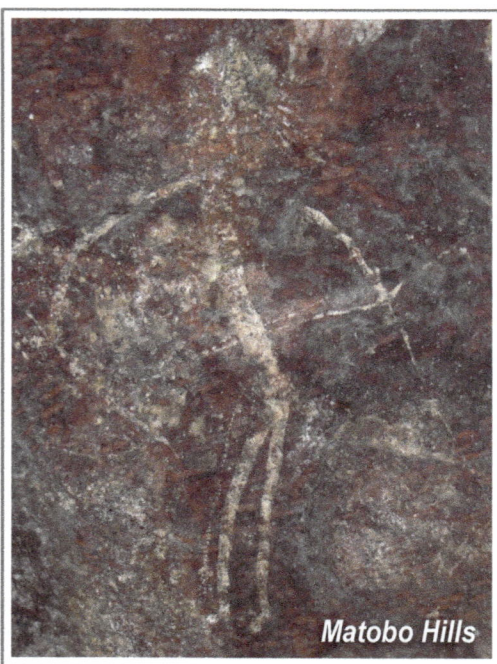
Matobo Hills

probably not surprisingly) zebra [p.74]. How these line images fit into the general chronology of the art has been debated, although without clear resolution, as to when and why they were done.

At some sites large paintings of animals and, less commonly, humans were crudely painted in layered white clay [p.70]. They were often painted in a prominent position in the larger caves, dominating the space in their apparent crudeness. These paintings are not, as people once presumed, more recent inexperienced copies of earlier art, or intentional defacement of the rock canvas by less skilled people. In fact they were a coeval element to the overall complex meanings portrayed in the panel. These so-called crude forms were socially meaningful, a nuanced statement which we mistake for inability.

When visiting sites we are often asked about how the art was painted so high up on the cave walls? Although unsaid, the questioner usually presupposes that the artists were "short Bushmen", incapable of reaching up high. This is wrong. Not all historical Sān were short in stature and most depictions are well within standard human reach. To paint the higher images, people used simple ladders consisting of lopped-off branches of trees propped up against the wall. In rare instances, these scaffolds can still be found in some of the more remote, less frequented caves. Their presence further supports our view that at least some of the art was painted fairly recently as the wood remains sound, it hasn't faced too long the ravages of time.

The extensive lower, smeared area found in many of the larger caves is perplexing and is probably the result of several things. Bodily contact by humans and/or kraaled livestock would unintentionally smudge the paint; natural body oils and sweat were rubbed onto the rock face and mixed with the remobilised pigment. In other instances, touching and smearing of the art may have been a deliberate social practice. The paint, like the images and the setting were all spiritually significant; the act of deliberately blurring the art may have been a way for people to ceremonially engage with the source of cosmological power behind it. Some authors have suggested that the smearing was done intentionally by later groups to hide or destroy the art. It may also be entirely natural in origin. The ashy nature of most cave deposits, together with microbiological activity on the rock face, results in the ultra-fine dust particles sticking to the walls through colloidal attraction, a physical bonding hard to break. It is probably a combination of all these causes.

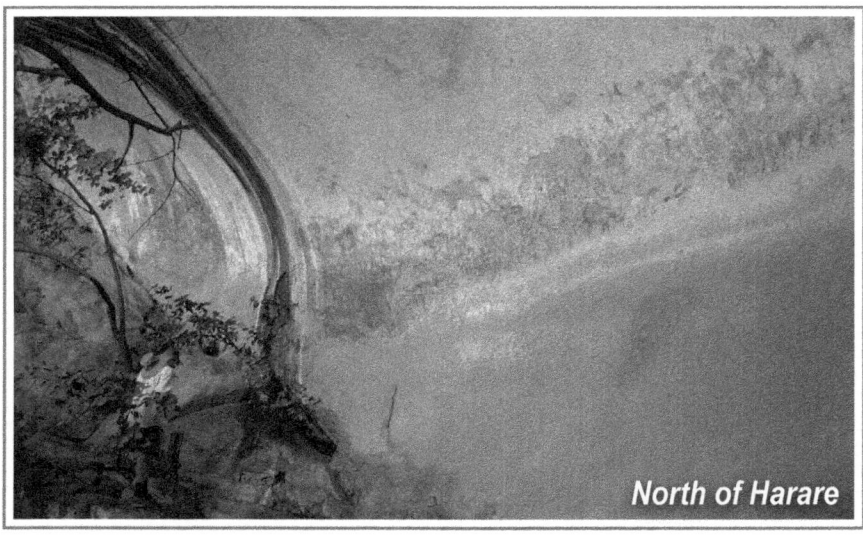

North of Harare

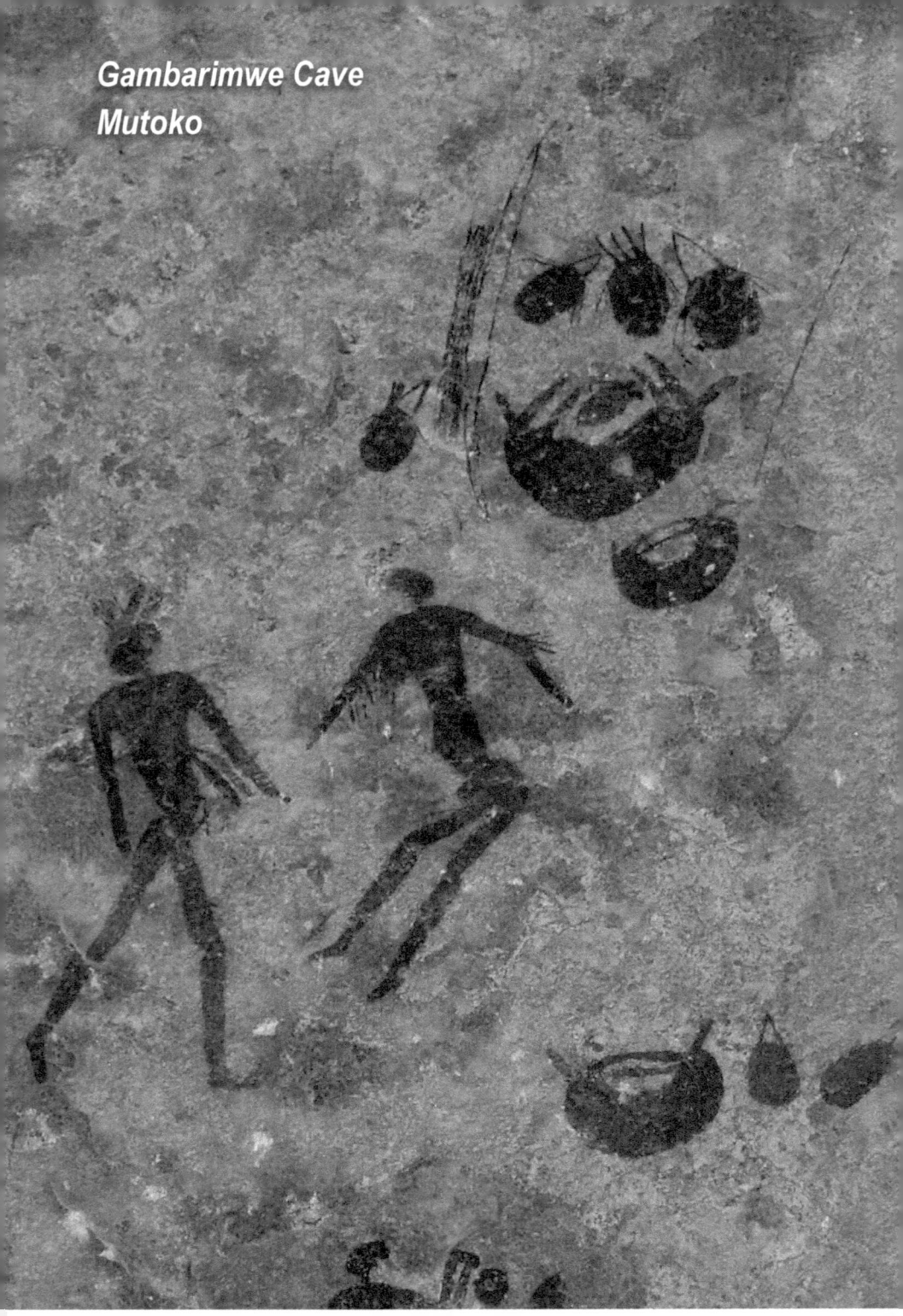

The Human Image

The rock art can tell us much about the past ways of life of the artists and their cosmological tenets. It gives us a glimpse into how people understood the complexities of life, interacted with each other as individuals and as a society, and how they related to the environment through that unique human attribute, spirituality. The art was created not simply for the enjoyment of the artists and their audience, but it had deeper meanings. It was a way of communicating, with those who once gazed at it, about the religious beliefs and practice, myths, magic and the laws of their society.

The meanings were undeniably complex as the painted images were multilayered, polysemic symbols, based on the literal as a point of referral. The forager artists, like all humans, drew upon their own everyday experience and imagination to transform reality as they lived it into symbols, images with social meanings. Sometimes these multiple meanings appear to conflict, and are dependent on the actual context. For this reason, it is extremely difficult for the outsider with a completely different cultural upbringing, to attempt to analyse the art. In this booklet, we offer some thoughts as to what we believe can be seen in our rock art, well aware that we probably fall short of the true depth of meaning that the complex communication once portrayed.

The first point we must stress is that our rock art is not one of realistic three-dimensional depictions. It is a tradition of drawing of distinctive profiles that pick out specific features of the object. As pointed out by the late Peter Garlake in his book The Painted Caves (1987:7), *'Outline was used to convey form, mass and solidarity. Through the outline of a silhouette alone, the artists described an animal or person.'* Through these images the Sān artists captured select human and animal qualities, representing an archetype of the species rather than the individual. We see the essence of the being, not the person/plant/creature.

The artists' preference for the side silhouette required the use of a twisted perspective so that horns, ears, shoulders, breasts and legs were shown at unrealistic angles to ensure that they appear. For instance, the warthog's head was usually depicted from above while the rest of the body is shown from the side; the crocodile's head was painted side on, while the rest of its body is shown from above; elephant tusks appear one positioned above the other, instead of being at the same level on either side of the head. What is clear is that the artists were more interested in depicting these, the quintessential characteristics of the object, rather than creating a realistic three-dimensional depiction.

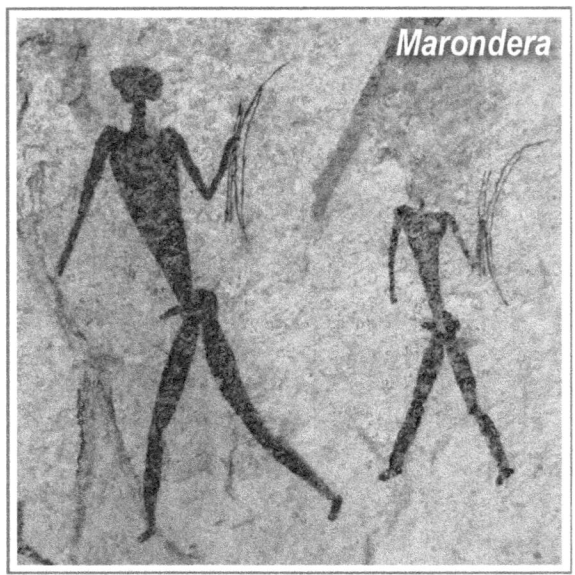

The association of any one image to others around about should not be treated as obvious. Extensive, and at times to our eyes confusing, painted panels should not be interpreted as one visual landscape, with each and every individual image related directly to those nearby. Some images were intentionally grouped, but others were created as isolated depictions within a mass with which they have no direct association. Unlike the western canvas, we should not seek to identify an overall composed landscape. The panel was a local creation by many artists over centuries. No sanctity was given to existing images, there was no private domain, no individual monopoly in creating the artistic composition which we now see. People happily painted or engraved across and/or next to the works of other artists. In so doing the artist was making his/her own statement to the observer, elaborating on or completely modifying the statements of the work others created before. The artistic panel was an evolving expression of socially-prescribed imagery, and we are fortunate to see the complex result.

Bodily Form

The human figures were depicted as all very similar; usually a basic naked profile and few individual features. Most human bodies appear twisted, with the heads, legs and genitals shown in profile, while shoulders, chest and arms were drawn from the front. In it we see the very essence of man and of woman, not the personality of the individual.

Generally males were painted more often than women, the genitalia being clearly depicted. However, many more human figures appear ungendered, although this can sometimes be deduced from the associated material artefacts and the activities in which these figures were shown. Quantitative studies indicate that, where gender appears, males were at least four times as likely to be portrayed as were women. This bias does, however, differ from site to site.

Some human figures appear as solitary individuals, independent *persona* depicted intentionally apart from all others. This is easily seen at smaller sites, but with larger panels it is much harder to grasp - which was an individual and which were part of a group? We, as outsiders, must never assume that the figures that appear to us as obvious clusters were intended to be related; all created all at one and the same time. Such group images could have evolved over hundreds of years as the panel was expanded, re-interpreted and redefined by successive generations of artists.

The bulk of human paintings show adults in their prime of life and the relative size of any one image to others nearby is no reliable standard as to different ages. The smaller painted figures are not necessarily children, but they may be.

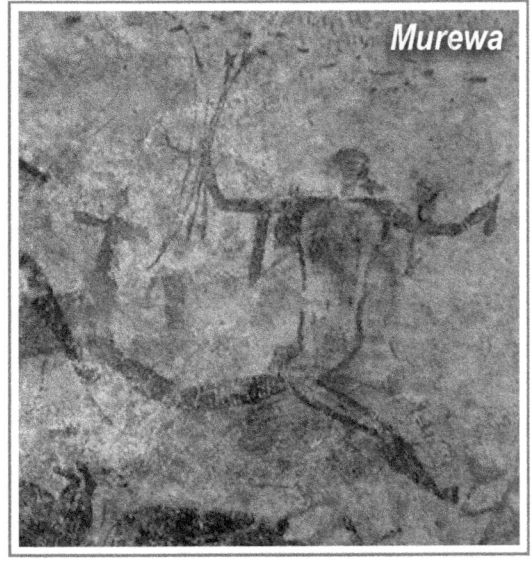

Most human figures appear standing or walking. Occasionally some appear running, their overstretched gait saying more about the notion of exertion and speed than a factual depiction.

While most human images capture correct anatomical proportions and shape, some images appear to be elongated, their twisted torsos

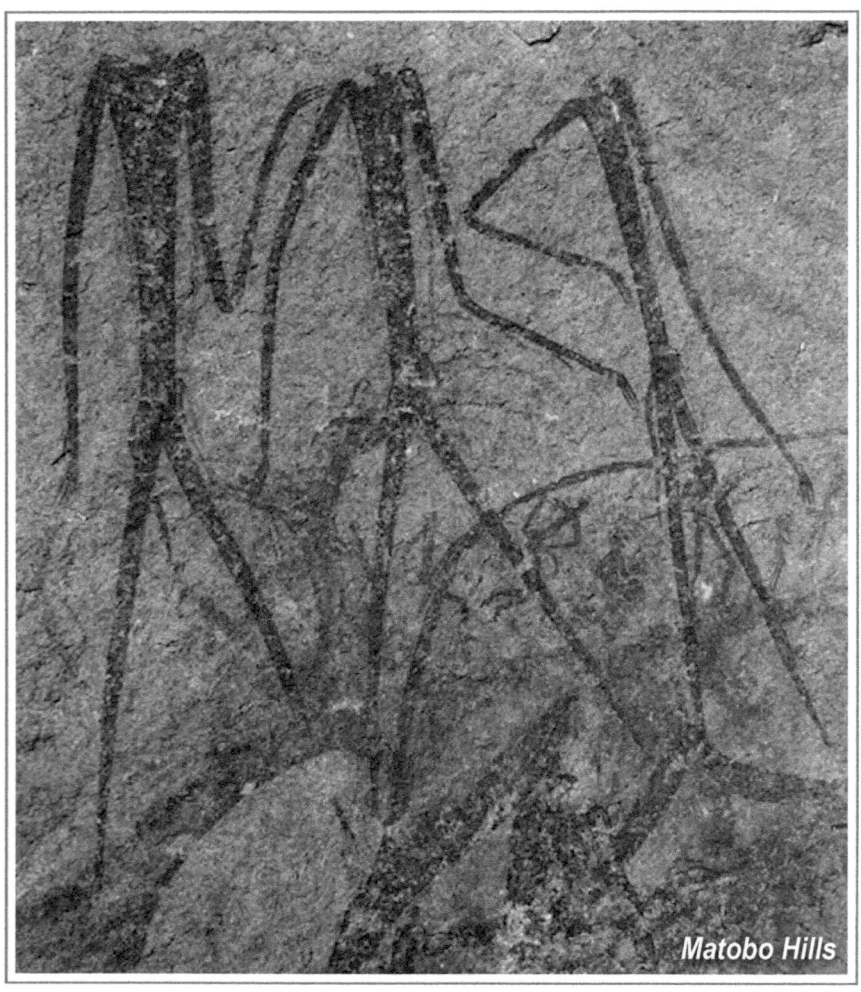
Matobo Hills

vertically stretched, over-inflating the width of the chest, the narrowness of the hips and the length of the arms and legs. The heads of many of these depictions were intentionally understated as mere rudimentary appendages. These groups are a particular feature in several of the larger caves of the Matobo Hills.

Elsewhere, apparently normal human figures are shown with excessively long arms and legs. Often spindly, these stick-like limbs were sometimes painted in completely unrealistic twisted perspectives. These creatures may not in fact be human, but could represent the spirits of the

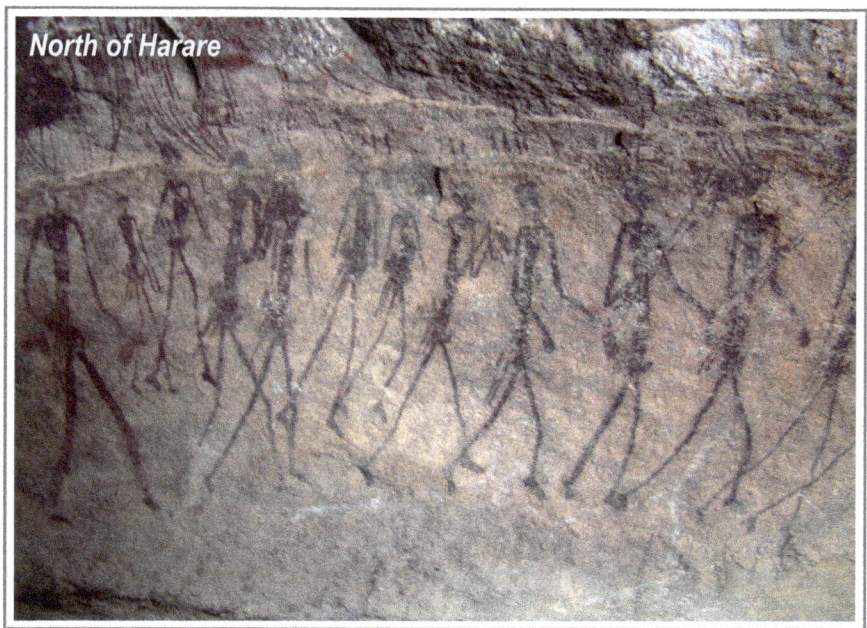

North of Harare

world that the present Sān informants say are ever present all around us at all times. Some of these spirits are said to be good/desirable; some evil/anti-social; while many more are simply there, neutral presences unseen in the landscape and air around us. Alternatively, these spindly forms could represent the soul or life power, the human essence which is said to escape from the body in both death and trance ceremonies [pp 57-61].

Looking closer, most human heads appear as blobs without additional features. Where the face was once painted in white, a shading now invariably lost through decay, the head appears as a rather strange hook. Other heads resemble the muzzled face of a baboon, while some have

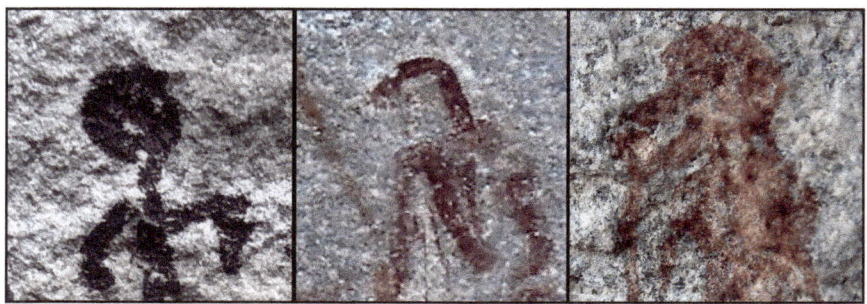

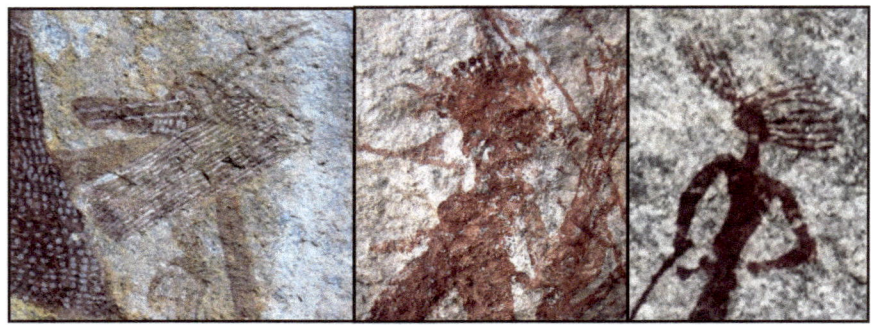

the ears and other characteristic features of antelope or, less often, felines. Many human heads have what appear to be hair styles or erect lines coming out of the crown or back of the neck. These lines could be literal representations, depicting hair spikes or sticks/arrows stuck within the hair. Alternatively, they could be representations at an abstract level, details conveying the sensation of rising hair and the *escape of the spirit out of the head*, experiences often described by modern Sān trance dancers. There may be yet other figurative meanings, making reference to the all-embracing creative power of the divine spirit that permeates the world around us. Possibly all of these meanings held true at one and the same time; interchangeable imagery in the minds of the artists and their communities where literal reality and abstract spirituality were inseparable concepts.

Human sexual organs, where shown, were invariably exaggerated. The female body was portrayed with two breasts, painted in profile one above the other, on the chest or lower down on the stomach. Many female figures also have enlarged, rounded buttocks. This may represent the physical condition of *steatopygia*, the localised accumulation of body fat in this area that can be witnessed in some Sān women. However, the overtly exaggerated artistic convention may have been more figurative than literal, expressing a Sān perception of womanhood. In a few instances, male figures appear with similarly exaggerated buttocks, putting to question any straightforward assumption as to the symbolic representation of sexuality. In such instances, the transgender elements of these images may have been intentional, imagery capturing the ambiguity of the ceremonial activity that was depicted.

Some female figures, often obese-bellied with legs shown stretched wide apart, have long lines extending from the vaginal area. This has been interpreted as a stylised portrayal of menstrual blood or birthing discharge. Such depictions could speak on both literal and symbolic levels. In many societies these basic female biological processes are socially-proscribed; they are defined as hot, dangerous and capable of causing social disorder. On a literal level, these depictions may record these important events and the associated social ramifications.

Alternatively, the apparent birthing depictions could be entirely symbolic, the imagery operating at a higher level of abstraction in the

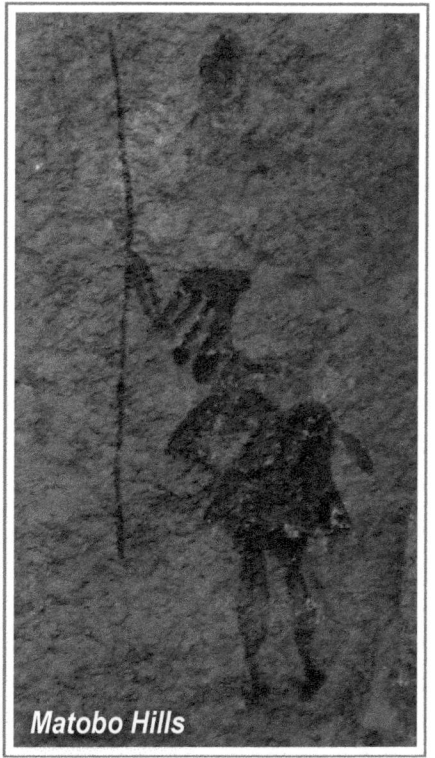
Matobo Hills

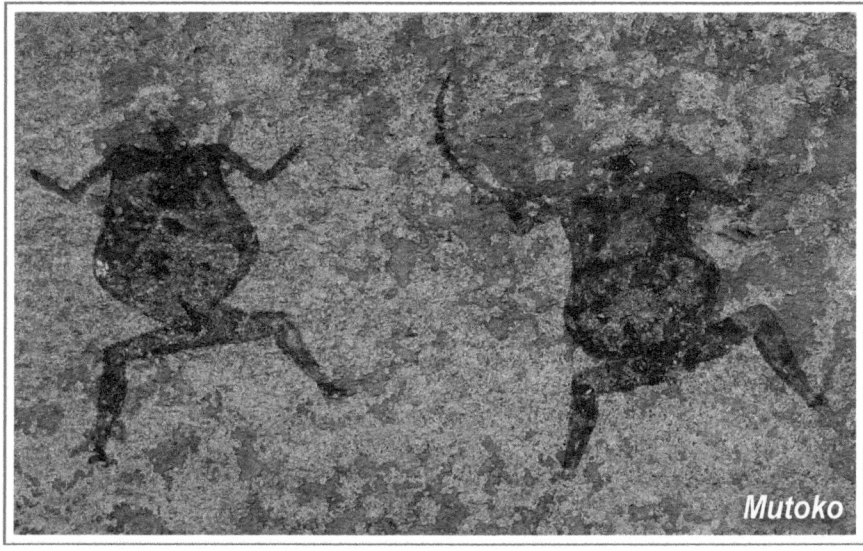
Mutoko

realm of myth and spirituality. We need to look closely at these depictions and those round about, especially where there are *lines of discharge* which often have smaller humans and animal figures attached. These imaginative, improbable scenes may have been statements of social norms concerning the role of women in society at large, and beliefs as to reproduction, creation and continuity of life in general. Particularly common in the rock art of Mashonaland, the paintings of large *fat women* not only acknowledged the assumed power of pregnant women, but they may represent a lot more, a version of the story of creation of all life, human and animal.

Most men in the art were depicted naked, although in reality they wore a small loin-cloth for modesty and protection of the genitals. This item of clothing is rarely indicated. Instead, the artistic tradition placed emphasis on the exposed erect or semi-erect penis. The scrotum is almost never shown. In many cases a *bar* appears drawn across the shaft of the penis. In years gone by, most authors described this as infibulation, arguing that it was a realistic representation of a stick/bone/quill that was inserted through the foreskin to prevent sexual intercourse. There is no ethnographic evidence for this suggested literal interpretation. It is more likely that this was a symbolic statement; the line representing social prohibition against intercourse at certain times, such as before hunting, while wives were pregnant or experiencing menstrual periods, or during certain ceremonial activities.

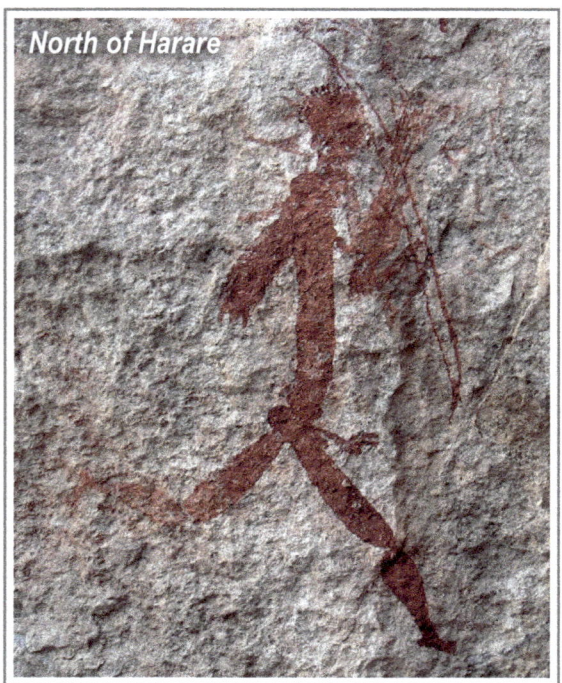

North of Harare

The presence of long *tassels* apparently hanging off or shooting out of some of the penises have also been

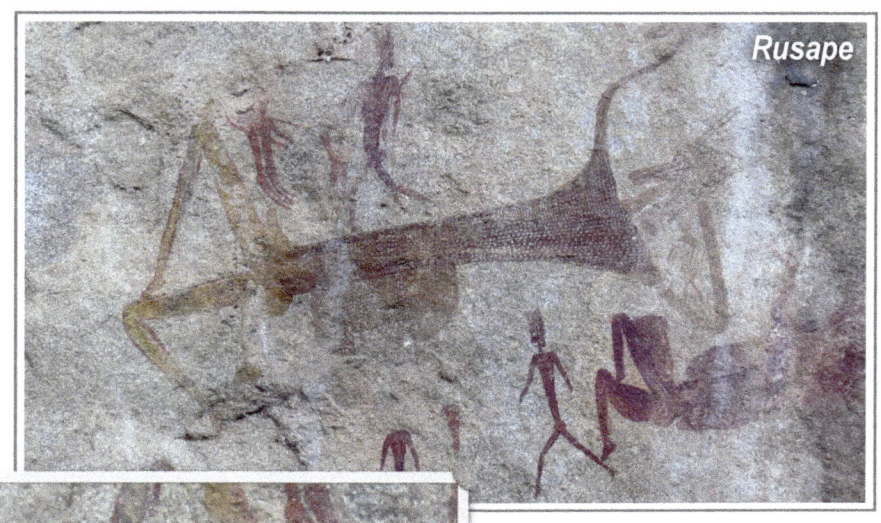

Rusape

misinterpreted. We don't believe that they are literal depictions of some ornamentation, such as a penis sheath. Instead, the *tassels*, some of which have enlarged ends, suggest to us that they portray the very essence of manhood, ejaculation.

Many human figures, both male and female, have short painted lines extending from the face, armpits or chest. These details could be both literal and symbolic. They may denote actual sweat and/or nasal blood. Both discharges, physical reactions to when the body is overheated, were/are considered especially significant by the Sān in their traditional ceremonies. Alternatively, the lines may represent an entirely abstract notion, as a statement of the spiritual awakening, boiling up and escape of the inner human spirit during death and social ceremonies. Confusing yes, but for the artists the diverse character of these entangled symbols combined both non-literal meanings and multiple literal associations.

Material Culture and Hidden Meanings

Although most human figures appear as simple, unelaborated profiles, some images have additional painted details of fine lines often done in white, but sometimes red, paint. These could be literal, representing actual body paint and/or strings of shell-beads and other ornaments. The latter were once, and still are, worn by both sexes in extant Sān groups, although today glass beads are more readily available. These painted strings of *beads* appear to ring the chest, arms and legs of many hunting figures and,

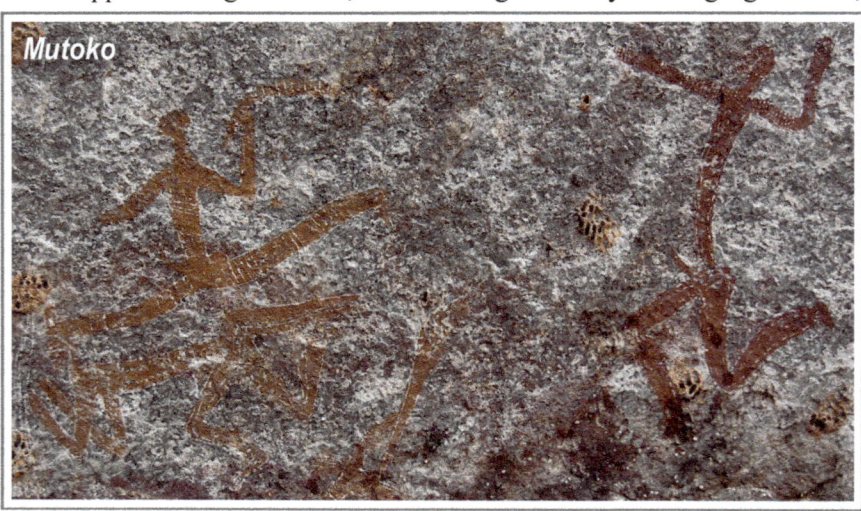

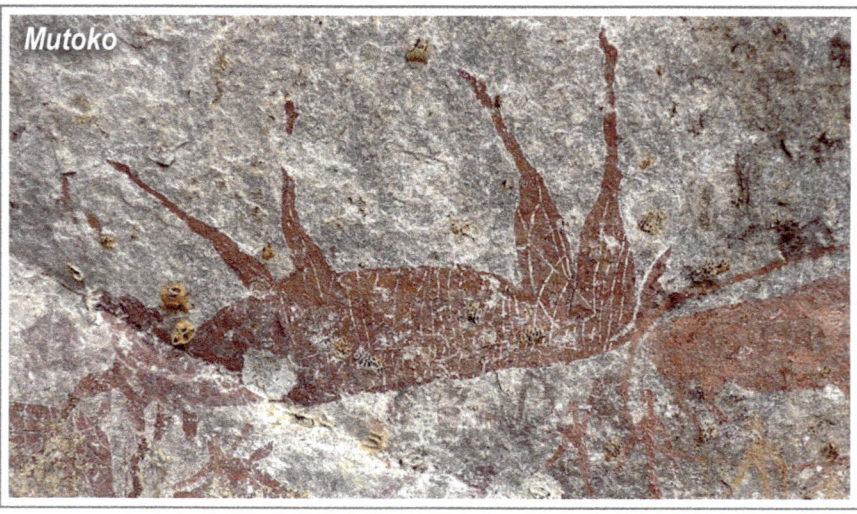

most curiously, of some images of wild animals where there is no equivalent as far as skin patterning. For this reason, we cannot accept an entirely literalist interpretation of these painted details. There are probably multiple meanings, combining literal referral and abstract notions. They may represent at one and the same time shell bead ornaments, as well as the sense of tingling felt in the body when overheated in the chase of the hunt, while dancing or during other ritual activities. Their inclusion on animal figures brings the latter into the realm of human experience, emphasising their complex symbolic nature. There may, however, be other meanings to these white dots and lines which we miss completely.

Generally very little clothing was shown. This is not because the people did not own much, but their absence was an artistic convention. One gets the impression that possessions were not considered as socially important as was the stylised, naked form of the human body.

Where clothes appear, women wear short leather aprons and/or tasselled skirts which cover/hide their buttocks, an element of the anatomy that modern Sān groups describe as particularly erotic. The differences in the shape and length of these painted skirts was intentional. Sān ethnography suggests that in normal circumstances older, married women wear longer, larger aprons and skirts so as to mask their sexuality. Unmarried women wear considerably less seeking to attract male attentions and marriage. Such statements as to age and sexuality undoubtedly appear in the art.

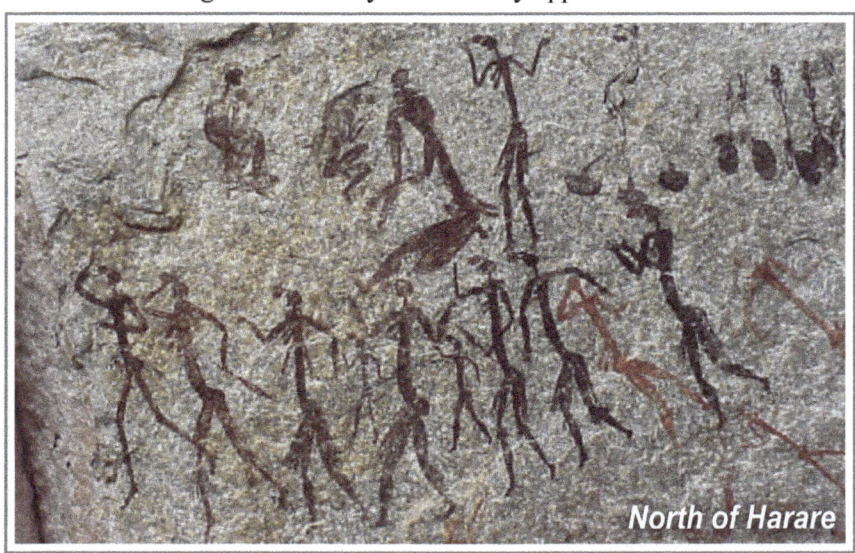

North of Harare

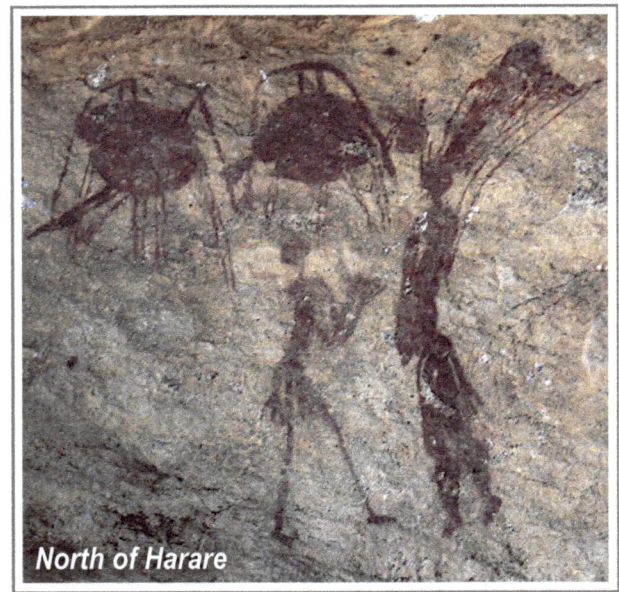
North of Harare

Other artefacts typically associated with women were skin bags. These were carried to the field to gather foodstuffs for the family, and as such, they are a direct statement of womanhood and their economic role as gatherers. Many gender-neutral figures associated with such bags are probably women, while in some cases the bag alone was painted, denoting its human associate. Given that these bags generally appear bulging, crammed with the product of the veld, so we have a statement of the feminine role as the nexus of family sustenance. It could also refer to the bounteous nature of the community's territory or *n!ore*, an underlying desire of all.

Skin bags may also have had other, less literal meanings connecting them with the uterus, pregnancy and childbirth. In both foraging and reproduction, the women ensured continuity of the family unit. The bag may also have been a metaphor for the trance dance. Modern Sān informants say that falling into an altered state of consciousness is like being captured in a bag. What may seem to us to be a simple, literal depiction of a utilitarian artefact, when painted it probably had multiple meanings to the artist's community, not necessarily exclusive.

Occasionally the female paintings have *skin tassels*, paired lines, extending from their arms, knees and calves (they also appear on some skin bags). These may represent everyday ornamentation, but there is possibly something more to it. They may portray things worn only at specific occasions, such as the ceremonies associated with the rites of passage of a young girl, or they may have been donned by women during the singing and dancing that was part and parcel of the trance dance. In such cases the representation is context-specific. Alternatively, these lines may be entirely abstract, expressions of divine power, *n/om* as described by modern *Ju/'hoan* informants. This energy, the very essence of all life, is said to enter or leave certain points of the human body during social activities. Again, what appears to be a simple, literal detail may have had much deeper, polysemic meanings which take the art to a higher level of symbolic expression.

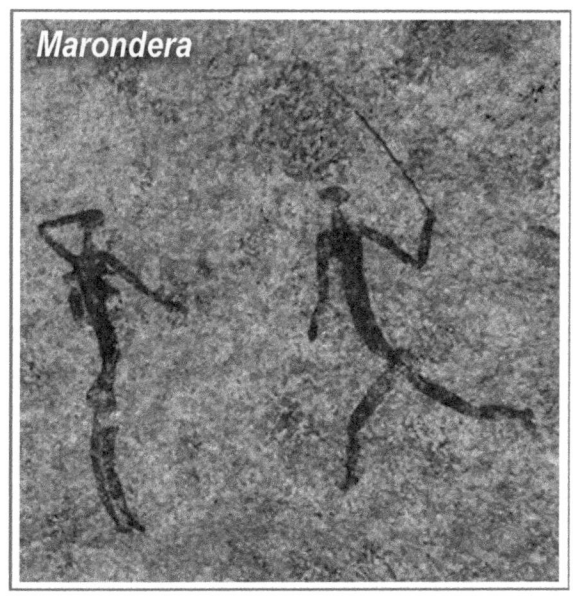

Marondera

The digging stick was another defining feminine artefact. This long, hardwood stick with a sharpened end was/is used by women to grub for roots, bulbs, corms, small rodents and termites, as well as to knock down fruits from the trees and open beehives for honey. Its presence identifies many of the otherwise gender-neutral images. Again, this artefact underscores the important female contribution to society and it is sometimes painted instead of the woman. The stick is also important in certain gynocentric dances and rituals. Sān ethnography also suggested that the stick itself is sometimes considered to be a metaphor for environmental wellness, the capacity of the group's territory/*n!ore* to support human activity. Once again the painting of the actual artefact had multiple non-literal meanings.

Most male figures appear naked, rarely do they show the small loin-cloth or apron which most men would actually have worn. Where depicted, the *skirt* on some male paintings looks remarkably similar to those shown on female images. This may reflect our own inability to distinguish the socially-understood subtleties painted by the long lost artists. We just don't see the real differences, or it may be that these were intentional cross-gender depictions. Today, in Sān communities, some

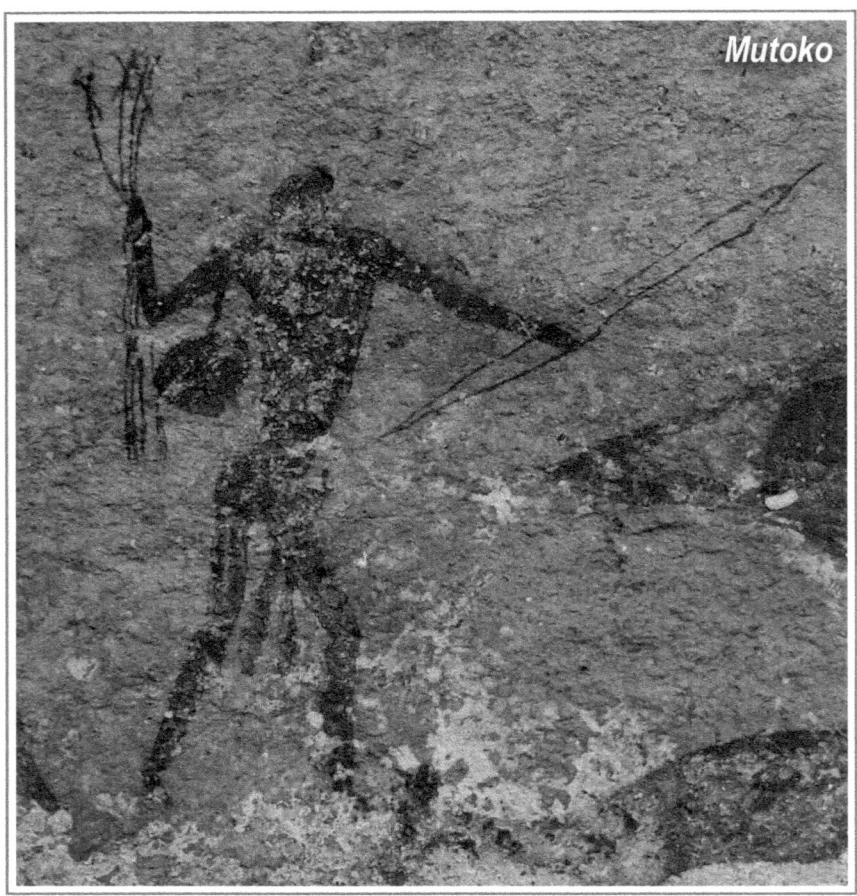

Mutoko

men will wear female apparel during certain ceremonies, a statement as to the ambitious nature of rites of passage and the trance dance. Maybe we should look more closely at the details and contexts of these confusing depictions?

Many of the men were painted with bows, arrows, spears, shoulder bags and quivers[5]. The inclusion of these artefacts underscored the socially-prescribed role of the man in Sān society where hunting provided the socially-desirable flesh which was shared with all members of the

---

[5] the bags were pliable animal skins, while the quivers were hard, cylindrical bark containers for the arrows. The quivers were usually carried secured inside a skin bag, with one capped end protruding to allow for easy access to the arrows when needed.

community over and beyond the immediate family unit. The association of these characteristic artefacts allows for gender identification in the absence of the obvious, while their depiction alone denotes the male presence.

In most of the paintings, the size of the hunting artefacts was inflated and we are no longer dealing with the literal. There is no evidence that long bows were ever used by Sān communities. What we see in the art are images of the traditional small bow intentionally exaggerated; they are underscoring the significance of these artefacts as part of the essence of manhood. In addition, many of the apparent arrow heads, the tip of the poisoned arrow that achieves the kill, are shown far too large or of a shape not actually used in hunting (large crosses or crescent-shaped tips). We need to appreciate that as artefacts the arrows probably had powerful meanings over and beyond the obvious, i.e. hunting of wild animals. Arrows bring about death, illness and transformation. They are also key elements in many androcentric ceremonies. In addition, many extant Sān groups describe the very act of hunting and the eating of meat as a euphemism for courtship and sexual intercourse. The exaggerated depictions of some arrows and the bows which shoot them hint at a gender bias towards men and their pursuits. The similarity in shape of some of the crescent arrow tips to the attachment bulges on the end of penis tassels is possibly no coincidence [p.39].

Some human figures, especially males but not exclusively, carry in their hands, or attached to other parts of the body, various curious shaped objects. Although not easily recognisable, these may represent rattles, fly-whisks, paint palettes, or other literal objects which were used in important ceremonies such as the trance dance. Modern Sān groups stress the fact that these artefacts enable the trancers to dance and fall into an altered state of consciousness. Other painted objects may have had some symbolic meaning, sadly now lost to us. These include strange crescent and spade-shaped objects that are often seen held or attached to the body.

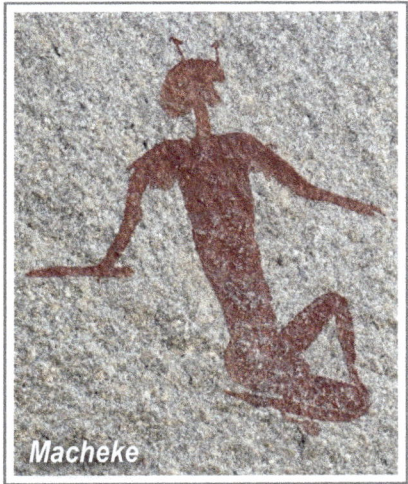
Macheke

Rather than a literal artefact these "objects", which the figures appear so keenly to hold on to, may represent abstract concepts encapsulating the power of trance and/or the "divine power", *n/om*.

Other figures appear to blow into long, rectangular objects, something akin to a blowpipe or a didgeridoo. We have absolutely no idea what these features represent. It is, however, a serious misuse of ethnographic analogy to suggest that they are one and the same as the traditional artefacts which are used by Australian and South American aboriginal groups. As with much of what we have already discussed, these apparent handheld "artefacts", coming from the mouth or heads of painted figures, may be more symbolic than realistic objects.

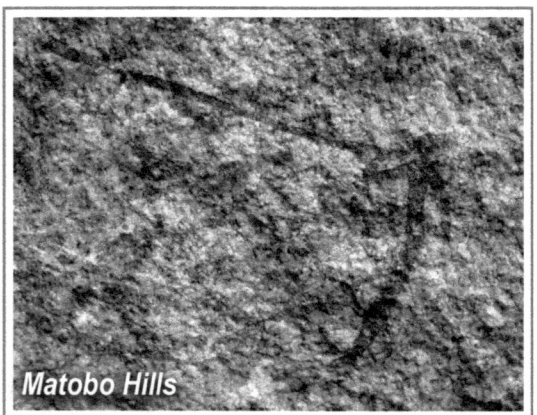
Matobo Hills

This is not to say that our artists' communities did not have musical instruments. For their many ceremonies and entertainment, the Sān are known to have used simple reed flutes, the musical bow, various rattles and maybe even drums (the last were probably a later adoption from farming community residents). Although never common, depictions of instruments that may have been used during certain ceremonies are known scattered throughout the country.

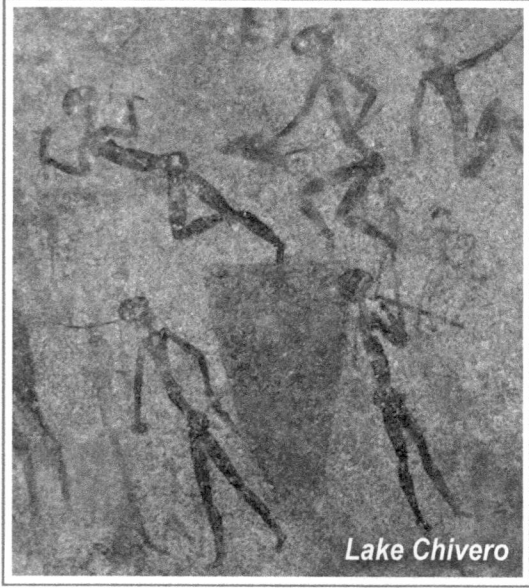
Lake Chivero

The Social Being

In the remote past Sān society was essentially egalitarian; all were equal except for limited social prestige afforded on the basis of gender and age. Older men were deemed the leaders, although this conferred little in the way of power over others. It is these social norms, socio-economic roles and ceremonies which are the basis of our rock art. It had a heuristic function. Through their depiction, community values were reinforced to those who painted and others who observed/read the resulting painted rock face.

Human groups were frequently depicted as lines of people walking or running, a literalist expression of the ceaseless movement of Sān bands across their territories, *n!ore,* in search of food, water, medicine and social interaction. The depictions reinforced this distinctive forager social norm. However, some groups painted in association with other symbols, such as large antelope-headed snakes, or with some individuals showing distinctive trance dance related postures, maybe in another dimension, in the realm of the spirits, where their motion may have continued, but at a symbolic level - visiting relatives in distant parts or chasing down game animals or the rain. Never prejudge, expecting the literal.

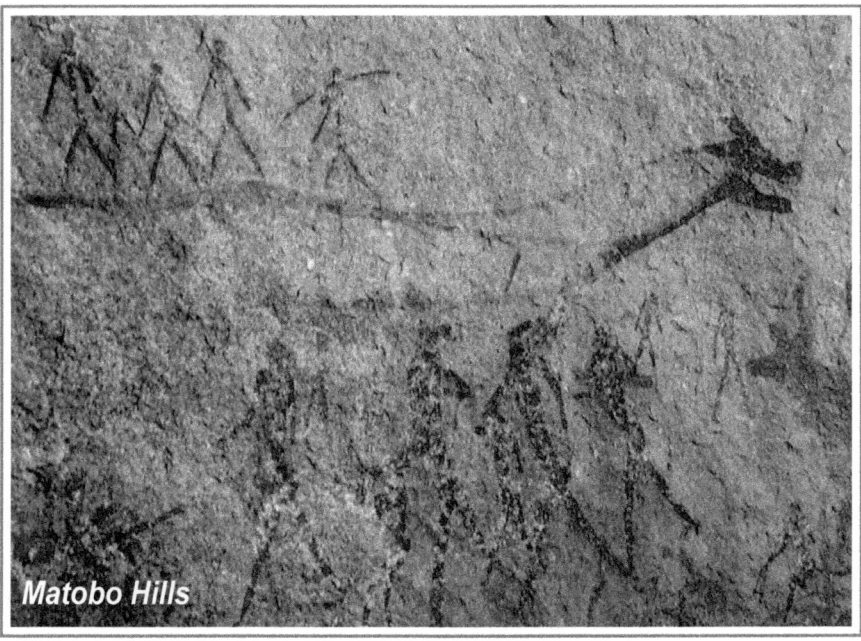
Matobo Hills

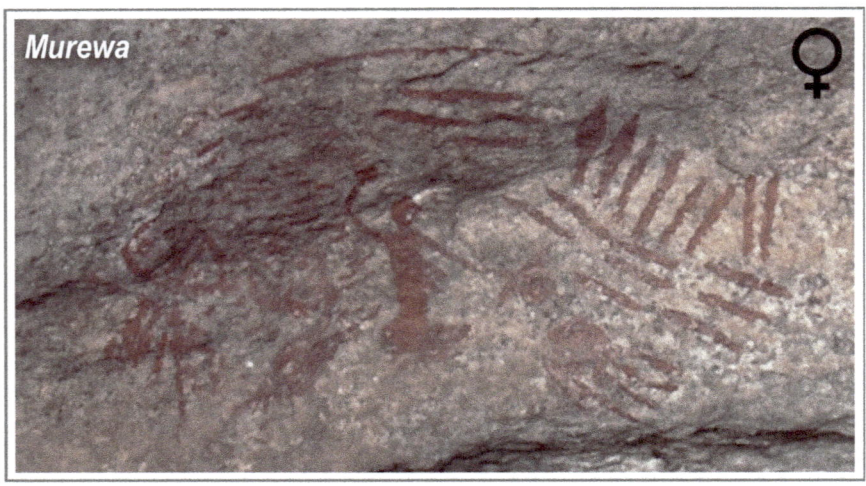

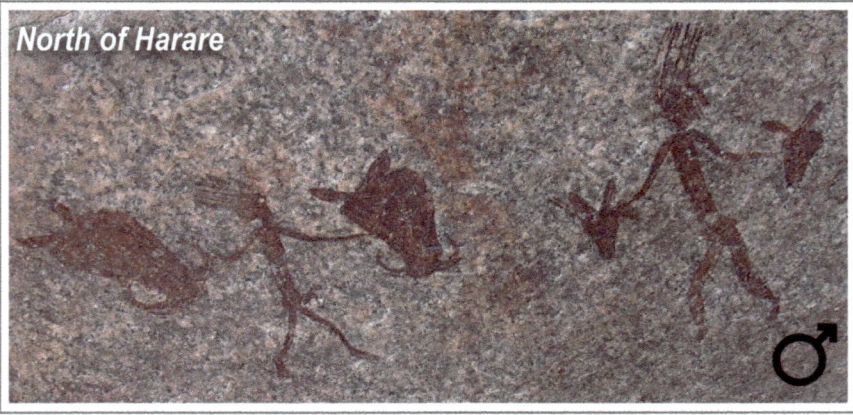

Women are often shown in their social role as the gatherer, provider of sustenance to the immediate family. It is of note, however, that plant, rodent and insect foodstuffs, and, by implication women themselves, are seriously underrepresented in the art. This is in marked contrast to the masculine endeavour of hunting which involved the shedding of blood and sharing of meat across the whole community. Deemed more socially desirable, the art thereby actively reinforced an androcentric world point of view.

Interestingly there are few unequivocal depictions of men trapping small game using snares or pit-falls, yet ethnographically these hunting techniques account for a good part of the male contribution to the community diet. Neither do we see people dismembering the carcass or sharing and cooking the meat. It is the hunt, and the hunt alone, that was considered socially significant.

At some sites, particularly the larger painted sites, we find fascinating domestic scenes. These depict the society's ideals of camp life showing gender-based activity, relaxation and the family/community unit. Occasionally small grass-built shelters are shown. These appear as multiple painted arcs occupied by human figures, a literal referral to the dome-shaped branch and grass structures that are still built today. While such scenes could be taken on a literal level, are they strictly domestic narratives? Are these not the visual expression of social-prescription whereby the rules of camp life were laid out so as to instruct the viewer. Also, when looked at more carefully, things are not necessarily so obvious. Often some of the human figures are engaged in ceremonial activities seemingly independent of the usual household setting. Other group scenes depict spiritual encounters with the "other", the spiritual realm which exists unseen all around us at all times. Again, through the artistic depiction, we have the codification of multiple social ideals.

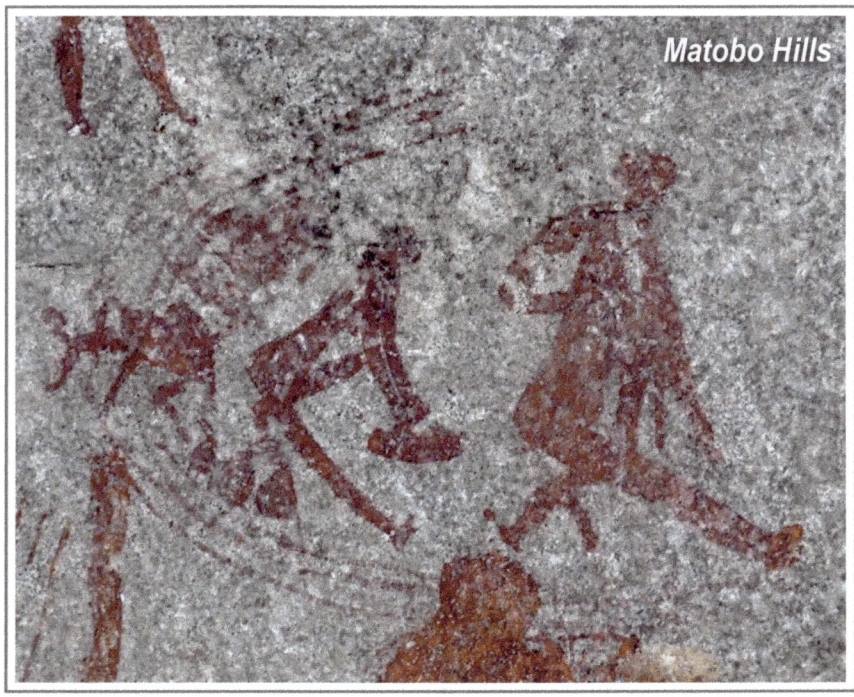

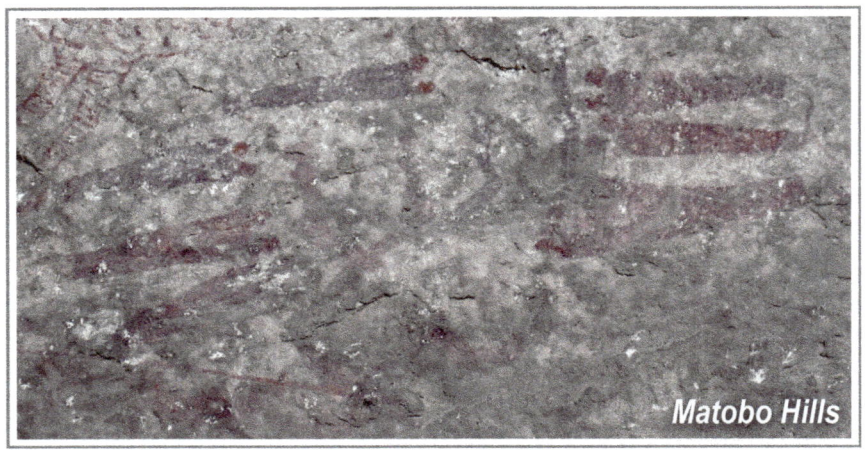

There are many scenes in our rock art which are decidedly raunchy. Pointing this out may offend some who either look away or condemn the art as the sketches of the *primitive savage*. Such attitudes say more about our own cultural conservatism than they do about the social meaning and intent behind the art. We must escape the trappings of Western Victorianism. In many societies sexual intercourse was not an embarrassing necessity, but was celebrated as the union of people and the proliferation of the community. That said, such scenes in our rock art are not pornographic narratives, but would have spoken to the Sān audience on wider issues of gender, marriage, procreation and children.

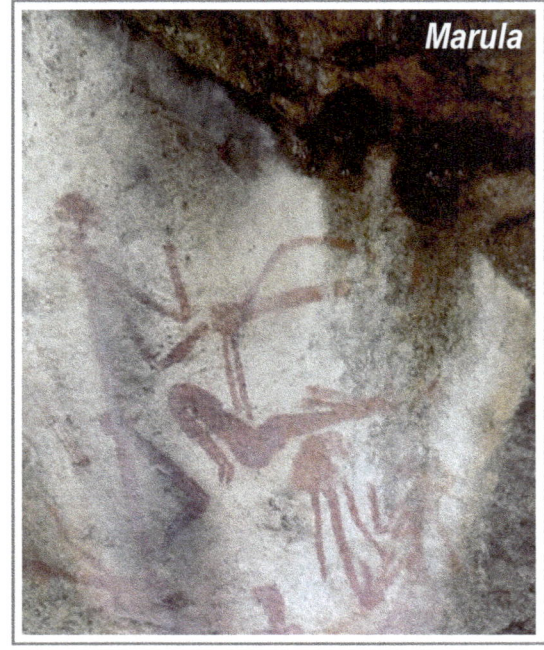

Many of these more lurid images appear part and parcel of group camp scenes, the couples often cocooned by what may have been a skin kaross. In other paintings the sexual act is fairly obvious. In other instances the same message may have been expressed through the joint painting of male and female artefacts. Similar statements of sexual desire and activity were expressed through animal symbolism. For instance, the postures of many kudu images are that of animal courtship and mating. Yet in such instances we are less offended, probably because we probably don't recognise the hidden meanings that were painted. In many cases, both on an obvious literal level and through symbolism, the art celebrates biological and social reproduction, something that would have been clearly understood by those who viewed and were tutored by the art.

Many painted group images, if not the majority, make reference to the various ceremonial activities which regularised these peoples' daily life. Ethnographic records indicate that all Sān groups believe in a *god force*, a divine power, that influences everything. It is described as an abstract, all pervasive power which is manifest in many things, so influencing individual humans and the experiences of the community at large. This life power is summoned and controlled during various ceremonies, often by select individuals who use it to bring about change or stasis in group dynamics and economy. This divine force is found in the land, air, rain, water bodies and in certain animals and people. Modern Sān groups have many names for it, *n/om* (Ju/hoan); *tssõ* (Nharo); ≠*ei* or *tçô* (Khwe). A social construct is the key to understanding our rock art. Its ceremonial summoning for both good and bad, and its ever present existence all around them, determined the routine of these peoples' daily life and their selection of many, but not all, painted images and symbols.

Important to all human communities are the beliefs and ceremonies associated with rites of passage, the ways people deal with (or ignore) changes in human status - birth; puberty and adolescence; marriage; divorce; and ultimately death. These are the liminal states of being, times of individual and social uncertainty, discomfort and transformation. It is at such times that people call on the divine to assist in bringing about change and restore social harmony. This is usually achieved through rituals, proscribed activities, and the discussions associated with these events. For our Sān artists, it is likely that the rock art was a powerful, visual communication, part of the social discussions associated with these rites.

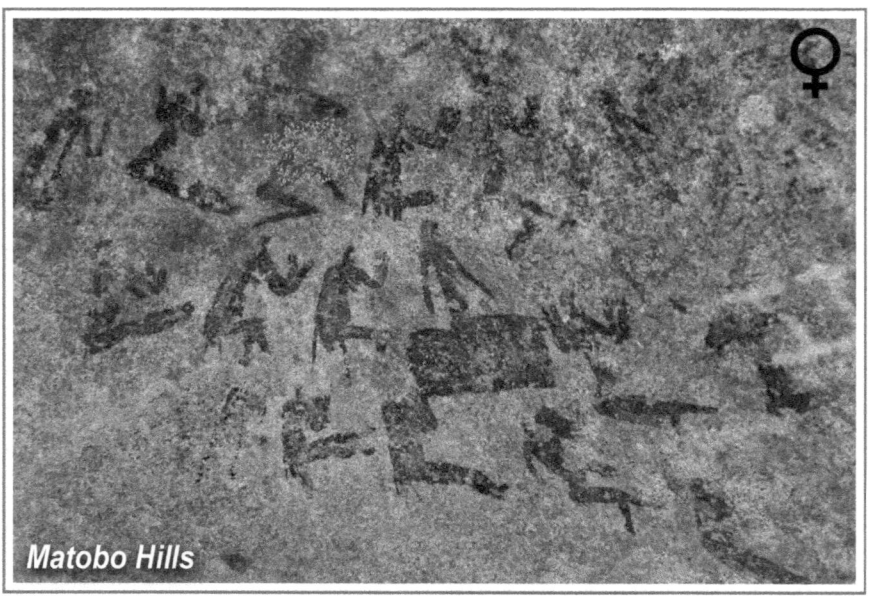
Matobo Hills

With this understanding, we can now look a little closer at many of the painted group scenes. The rites of passage of the adolescent girl is a fairly common, easily identified depiction. Here groups of women, with the occasional man, are shown clapping while seated or dancing with or around a younger woman, the neophyte, who is the subject of the ceremony of social transformation. Ethnographic Sān groups say that the songs of this ceremony activate the divine power thereby assisting the young girl in her bodily change from being a child to a woman capable of marriage and child birth. It is said to be a time of extreme danger, social ambiguity and potential individual discord that could destroy the entire community, dangers avoided through ritual.

These female rites of passage can appear as obvious narrative groups, such as that shown above, but they may also be more subtle, obscure to us with our untrained eye. Lines of women often may show subtle differences allowing us to isolate the young neophyte amongst them. This could be the shape and position of the breasts; the size and position of the aprons/skirts; or the central position and posture of one of the figures which is clearly the young woman, focus of the ceremony. The late Edward Eastwood, who spent a considerable time studying the art of the Limpopo Valley, noted that often the participating female figures are partially transformed, depicted part animal with their legs reversed at the knees as is the case with antelopes, or legs ending as wedges which he believed represent hooves. Basing his arguments on Sān ethnography, this, he claims, is the result of the songs of power used during the ceremony which called on specific animal spirits that embodied the transforming power of the divine life spirit. We can now look more closely at the subtleties of the different figures which make up the line of women shown on p.41.

In Sān communities the young boy's initiation was a less social affair, but it was no less important. Generally it required the *first kill* of an animal of size. Existing groups talk of the need to kill an eland, although this has rarely been observed by ethnographers, and what people say and what actually happens at the end of the day may be two very different things. What is important, however, is that the young boy, on showing signs of sexual maturity, was isolated from the rest of the community where he was instructed by the elder men on the man's role in society. He was then sent out to make his first official kill, his rites of passage. This ritualised event showed his ability to provide for the future family and for the community at large. During this hunt the adolescent acquires the sexual potency of the all-pervading divine power, transforming him both physically and socially.

We suspect that some of the apparently obvious hunting scenes in our rock art are no simple newspaper account of successful hunts. Just as with paintings of the girl's rites of passage, these apparent narratives were

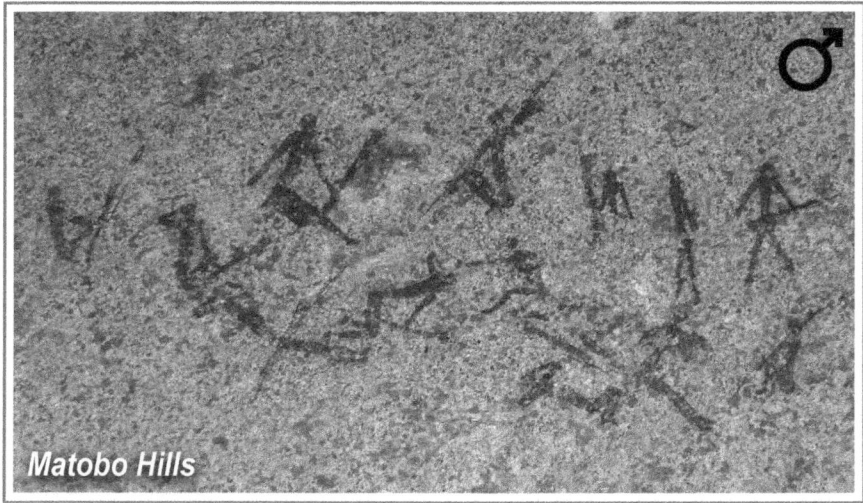
Matobo Hills

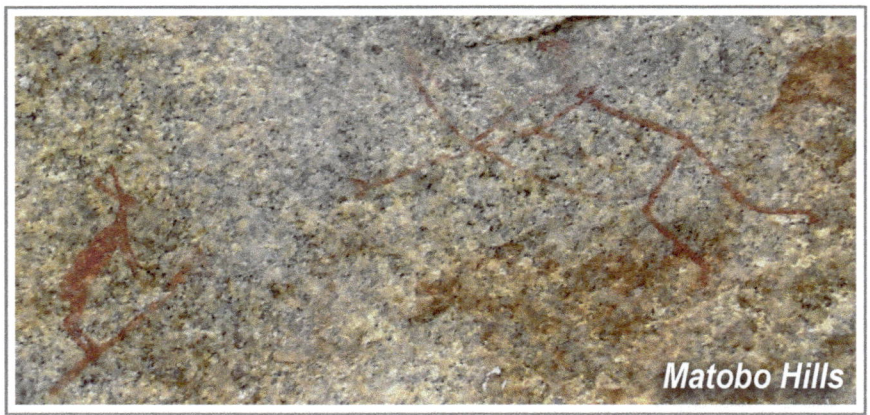

social statements of transformation of the neophyte. They were a means of instruction for the benefit of both the individual and the community at large.

Other hunting scenes probably had completely different meanings and one needs to pay particular attention to details of the prey, whether it is group or individual activity, and undoubtedly additional subtleties that we, the uninitiated, don't discern. While paintings of group hunts are known, never really common, closer inspection often reveals something deeper. They are more than literal narratives capturing the very excitement of the

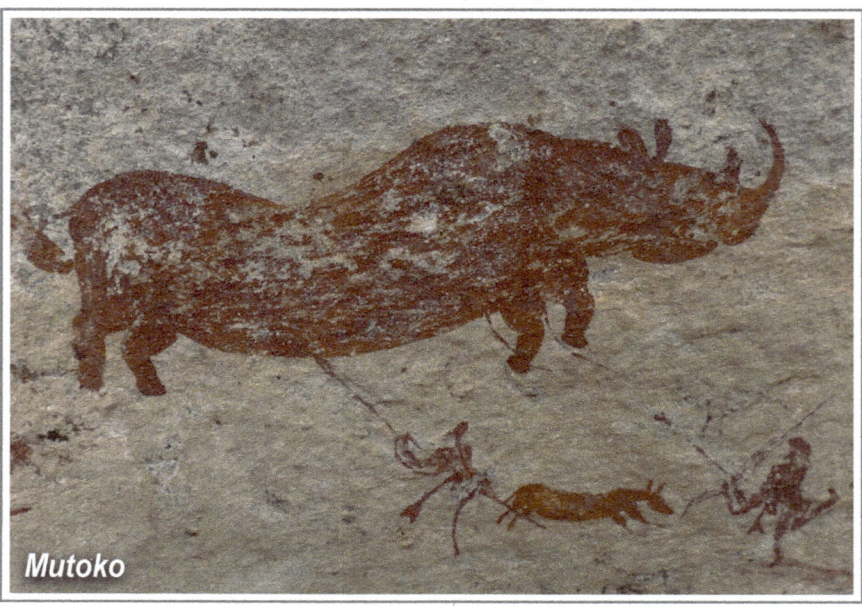

chase. Most unmistakable group hunts involve large, potentially dangerous animals such as elephant, rhinoceros, hippopotamus and the large cats. Given the technology of these ancient, Sān hunter-gatherers, it is unlikely that they would successfully kill the first three opponents. Their wooden spears and stone-tipped arrows would have had minimal impact on these mega-animals of the African landscape. Even those group scenes involving animals regularly hunted are probably symbolic hunts, asserting the very desire for success of man the hunter.

There is probably a lot more to these apparent hunts than meets the uninitiated eye. As will be discussed in the next chapter, the animals themselves were symbolic. Many were considered as animals of the rain, and by implication their hunting, both literal and in the symbolic realm, promised plenty of meat and thus social satisfaction. In other instances, the animals portrayed were a threat, they symbolised a potential danger that needed to be hunted down and destroyed to ensure the very fabric of human society. It is likely that most of these hunts were not narrative but figurative, expressing social desires and concerns. When looking at the art, do not be too easily swayed towards accepting the obvious.

The very same circumspection applies to the apparent fight scenes which are fairly common. Some of these paintings involve individuals, while at other times different groups are pitted against each other. Again it is highly

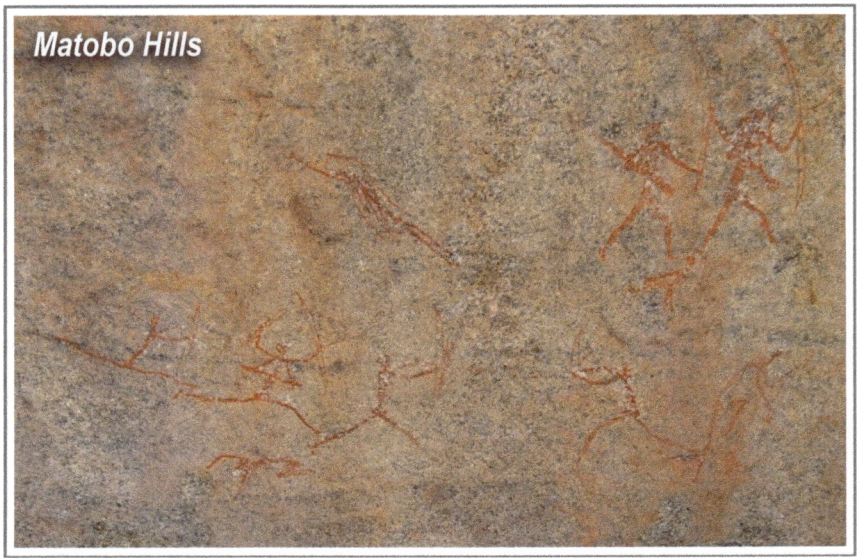
Matobo Hills

unlikely that we are dealing with a narrative. There were probably multiple meanings, not necessarily exclusive. The fights could be the community against the unwelcome spirits that exist at all times in the world around them; they could be metaphoric of the anger and distress experienced during rites of passage and the important trance dance ceremonies of the Sān; or they could be a statement of potential discord, something that was depicted in the rock art to forewarn the viewer.

Another fairly common artistic representation of potential social discord verses co-operation appears as linked pairs of both human and animal figures. Sometimes the juxtaposed pairs face each other, while an adjacent set is intentionally portrayed facing apart. In some cases one linked pair is human, while the opposing combination is another animal. It has been suggested that those individuals shown facing represent the socially desirable virtues of co-operation, unity, and community cohesion, while those facing apart depict discord, social danger and the isolation of the individual - things to be avoided. This paired symbolism was sometimes reinforced through the addition of a "pole", a line shown linking the two figures walking apart, towards each other, or in the same direction.

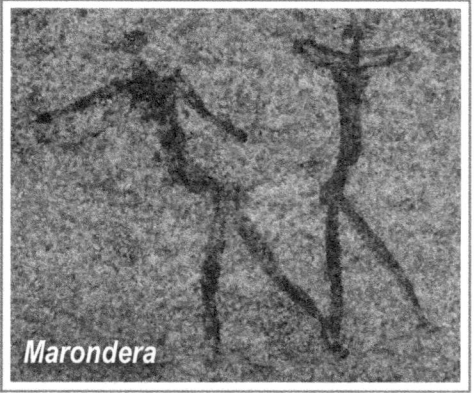

An important group ritual practice, one of the central pillars of Sān ritual life, was the

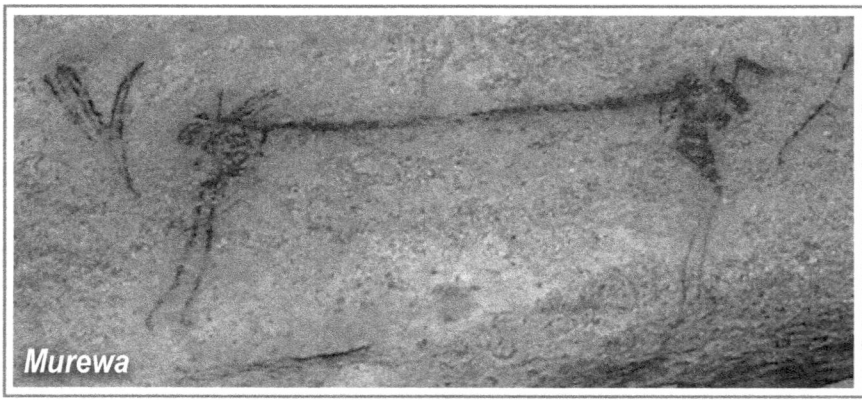

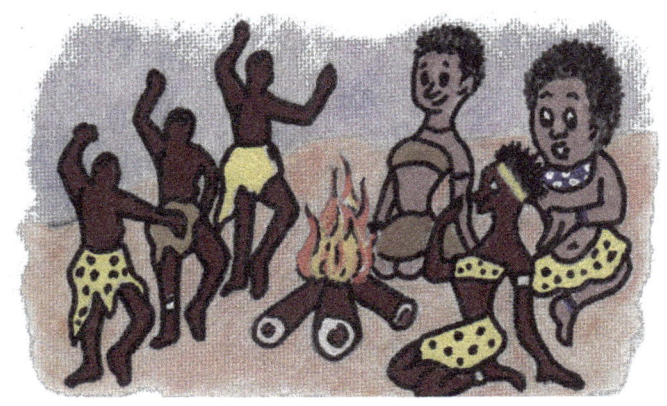

The "Sān Trance dance", cartoon by the the late Sininisabo Tshuma

trance dance. Ethnographic studies have shown that this ceremony and the experiences of the shamans involved are often inseparable from all other social activities, mythology and the Sān worldview. Together with stories of explanation, this activity defines the people, their beliefs and the events of their daily lives, something we have already hinted at. While a feature of contemporary Sān groups, it is likely to have considerable time depth in some form or other; transcendental experience is common across many foraging societies as people seek to rationalise the cosmos around them.

Before pointing out this ritual activity as it was painted, it is helpful to first look at the trance dance as practised by modern Sān groups. Held regularly, but most especially during times of environmental and climatic stress, social discord, economic anxiety, physical and mental illness, and associated with rites of passage, the trance dance brings together all members of the community. The dance and the subsequent public discussions of the shamans empowers the community; reasserting social roles, rationalises and overcomes the daily uncertainties of life, and provides the people direction in their social and economic life.

Today most shamans are men, although women are not unknown. It is considered a social privilege and the individuals are greatly admired as the trance experience is a dangerous, uncomfortable one as they sink into a semi-conscious state. It is said that the shamans temporarily die in the process, exposing themselves to the terrifying and uncontrollable visions and pain associated with their transcendence into the spirit world. It is in this detached state of mind that the shamans are believed to perform good deeds on behalf of the community.

The trance dance usually happens at night, people gathering in an open place, in the past probably in some of the larger caves. Here a large central fire provides light and heat to the proceedings which may last many hours, if not throughout the entire night. The women, children and elderly sit in a wide circle on the outside or are clustered nearby. They sing and clap rhythmically, while an inner ring of dancers, often adorned with rattles and holding ceremonial fly-whisks, shuffle around the fire. The undulating chanting, constant motion and heat of the fire will, with time, induce experienced shamans to hyperventilate and fall into an altered state of consciousness, into trance.

At this point several involuntary physiological experiences occur, some of which are depicted in the art. The shamans experience sharp muscular contractions, especially of the stomach muscles, and they violently bend forward, throwing out their arms before them in an effort to keep balance. They mention feeling a burning tingling throughout their entire body, while their limbs feel as though they are violently stretched and their head and hands shrink. Involuntarily, the shamans sweat profusely and sometimes experience nasal bleeding. These fluids are often rubbed on people to achieve social and physical healing. With further dancing, some of the more experienced shamans fall to the ground, muttering and oblivious to the real world around them. Occasionally they land in the central fire and get burnt, but are assisted when necessary by non-trancing

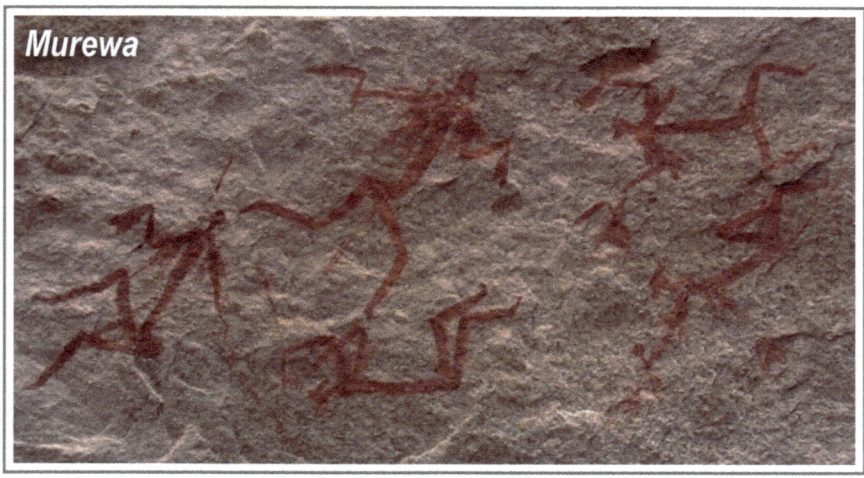
Murewa

participants. All of these physical manifestations of trance activity can be found in our rock art - dancing groups or individual shamans who often hold whisks and rattles; figures bending violently forward with out-thrown arms; modified limbs; and thin lines representing sweat and nasal blood.

Falling deeper into *death*, subconscious, the shaman's very spirit is said to boil in the stomach and rise up through the spine to leave the body from the head or the point where the skull is attached to the backbone. This feeling of tingling in the body's main nerve system is represented in the art by the thin lines shown emanating from the head of painted figures, often misinterpreted as a hairstyle [p.36].

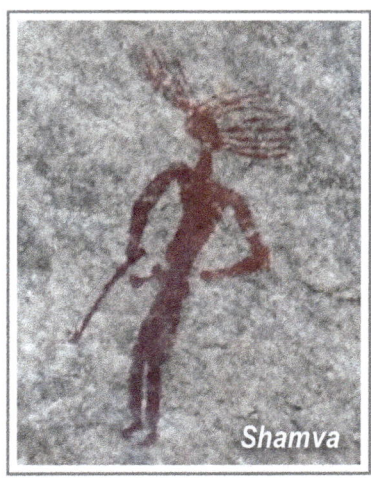
Shamva

At this point of self-induced trance, the shamans say that they cross a boundary, a curtain, into another realm. They enter into a blurry *other world* of chaos dominated by spirits - animal; fellow humans as well as their own spirit body; unknown life forms, often wraith-like; and other abstract forms (blobs, flashing lights and lines). This transcendence is, they believe, achieved by drawing upon the divine power of their setting and from certain animal spirits, subjects of the songs sung at the dance in question. In some instances, the shamans say that there is a fusion of their own spirit with those of the animal spirit whose divine power they have exploited. This common explanation accounts for many otherwise curious half-human and half-animal images, the therianthropic paintings which can be found in our rock art.

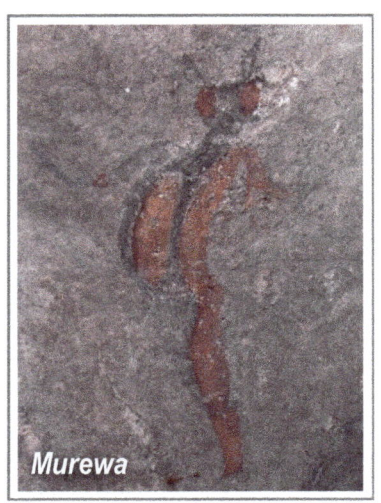
Murewa

Having now *escaped* from the mortal body, the spirit of the shaman is

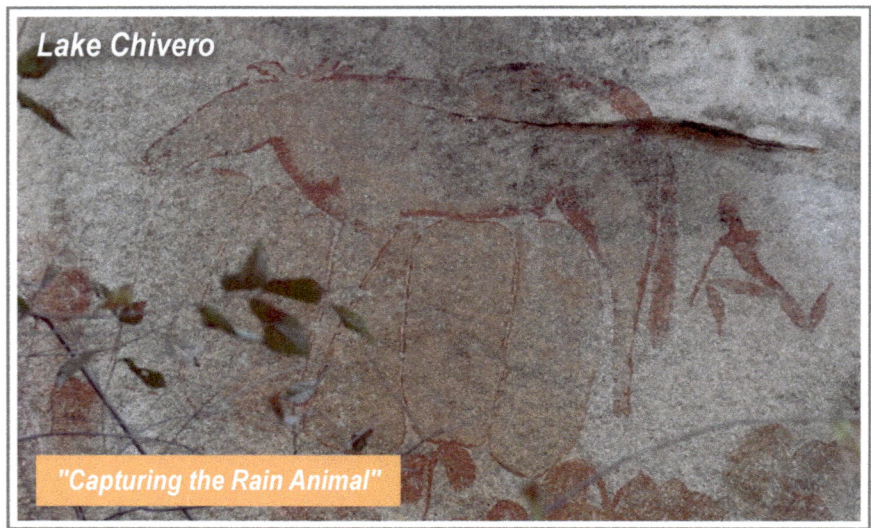

Lake Chivero

"Capturing the Rain Animal"

said to move through time and space doing good works - driving off evil and misfortune; checking on distant relatives in other territories; drawing the game to the hunters so ensuring success; capturing and bringing towards themselves the various manifestations of the *rain animal* (rains ensure plant foods and fresh food for the hunted animals); while they heal the heart/soul/body of those in their community in the "real world". Many apparently literal scenes in our rock art probably recall these spiritual journeys in this *other world*.

After some time as their bodies cool, the shamans will gradually recover, awakening from *death*. During this time they are closely cared for by the community. All are said to be in extreme danger. As with the rites of passage, this is another time of extreme physical and social ambiguity which they say will destroy the entire community unless the transition from one state of mind to the other is handled with care.

Much of the social consolation and community cohesion that results from the performance of the Sān trance dance is generated by mutual participation in the event, but more especially through the discussions that happen later. Shamans describe their experiences, sometimes debating amongst each other as to what was seen in the other realm and which spirits they encountered. Even those who did not go into trance are fully engaged and lessons are drawn from the experiences of the shamans. Through talking, a social catharsis assists to put aside built-up tensions, peoples' respective socially-proscribed roles are redefined, and climatic and economic concerns are seemingly addressed. Following the revelations of the dance, the people fully believe that the rains will come; the hunt will be a success; and that distant relatives and friends are faring well. Any negatives are put down to the presence of other, as yet evil forces, necessitating further trance dances.

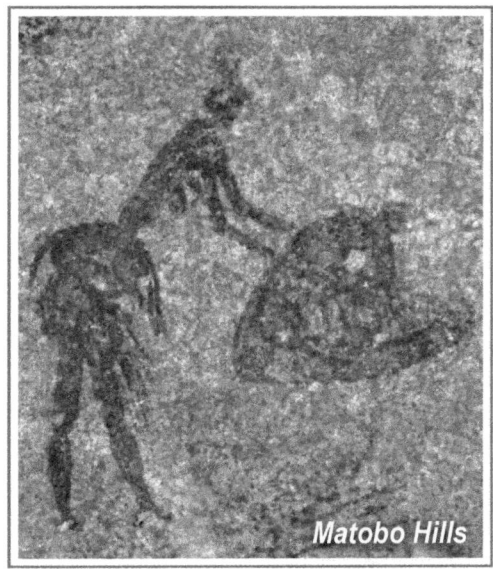
Matobo Hills

It is thought that much of our rock art was a similar means of communication narrating the trance experience. It was a more permanent, visual expression through which the shamans' experiences were recorded for all in the community to see and understand.

The trance dance ceremony, while a key activity in Sān society, should not, however, be treated as the sole explanation of our rock art. We feel that this is an over simplification which has appeared in the literature, a reductionist approach which undervalues the complex worldview of the artists themselves. One of several ceremonies, the trance dance and associated shamanism operated within the general social structures and symbolism of the community. They use these symbols, but are not the sole determinant of them. To appreciate our rock art more fully, it is necessary to adopt a more holistic approach, teasing out the nuances of symbolism, itself a complex and independent social construct, and understanding the activities/practices in which these symbols operated, be it trance; mythology; culinary protocols; gender and sexuality; rites of passage; material culture and speculative thoughts as to spirituality. All are interlocking elements of the human condition, no one part overriding all of the others.

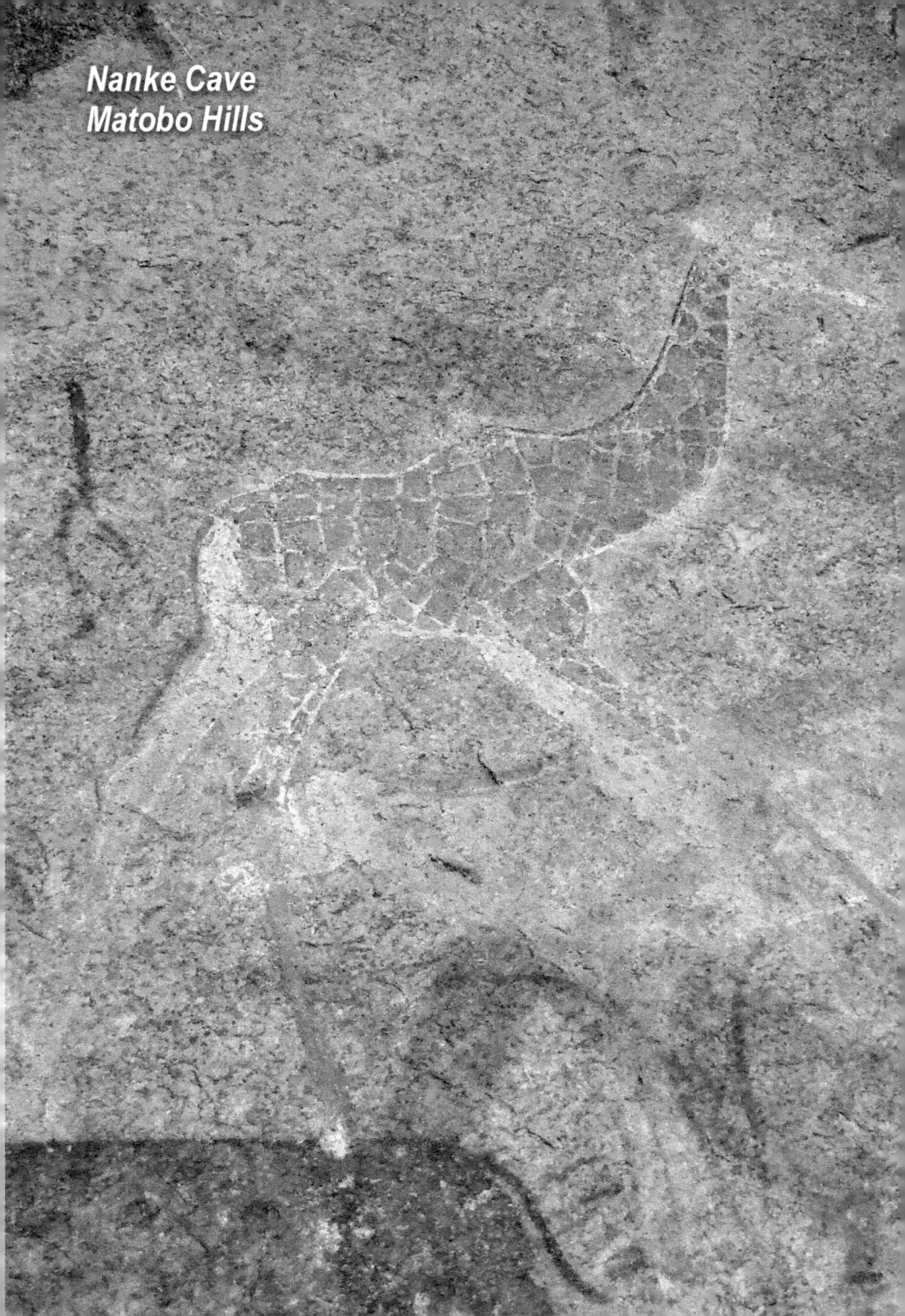

The Animal Symbol

Wild animals were an important element of sustenance in the daily lives of Zimbabwe's early foraging communities, but they were also symbols. Animals were a medium used to think, to categorise and explain. Their representation in the art was more than mere representation or reduced to sources of trance-inducing power.

Usually animals were well portrayed, better than the stylised human figures which feature in our rock art. However, not all species appear. Only certain creatures of the wilds were shown, those that the artists' culture selected as symbols, meat for the mind and not necessarily the body. Ethnographic studies and the bone remains recovered during archaeological excavations indicate that smaller animals were important sources of meat - impala, duiker, dassie, rodents, tortoise, reptiles and insects. Yet these species were infrequently depicted in the art. On the other hand, certain medium-sized to larger mammals appear over-represented. Clearly there was a socially-prescribed selectivity in what was, and what was not, shown.

As may have already become obvious in this booklet, traditional Sān do not readily differentiate between the natural/literal and the abstract and supernatural. Both states are intertwined, inseparable. There is, and there was, no distinction of the bipolar opposites of science and religion, myth and reality, nature and humanity.

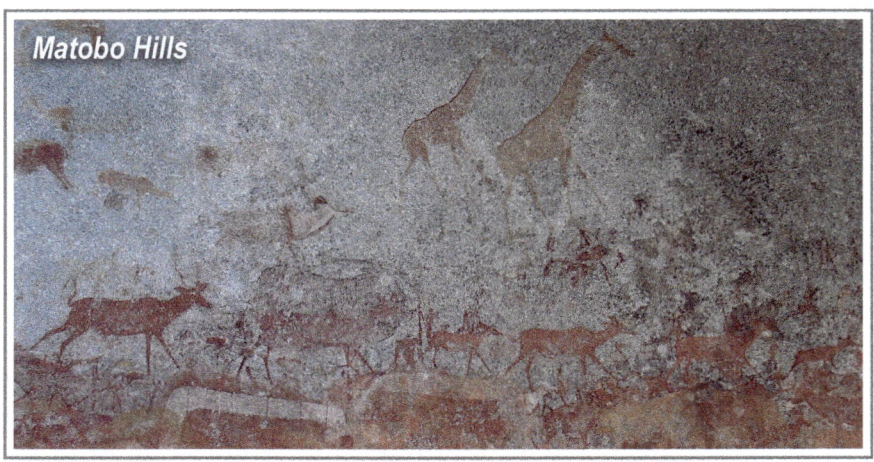

The Forager's world - a montage of animal symbols

We believe that the animals depicted were socially-proscribed symbols, selected to narrate and explain human values and aspirations. The animal symbols dealt with the fundamental questions of individual and social life, matters such as age, gender, happiness, sorrow, fear, sexual intercourse and the general human concerns as to the meaning and direction of the cosmos. As our worldview is so markedly different, we are outside of these artists' cultural frames of reference, it is not necessarily easy to recognise and understand what these associations were.

For some readers, the very idea of deeper meanings may be hard to accept. Yes, we agree that the art is delightful and that many animals are beautifully depicted, but what we see is not literal. The painted rock face was not simply what they saw in the bush. These people had a close, daily experience of nature around them. They would have observed the most minute facets of animal behaviour and bodily characteristics, many of these would have been given human meaning. Specific animal behaviours, such as walking, lying down, feeding, running away in alarm, courting and breeding behaviours, and aspects of birth and death, would have became points of referral; abstracted from the world of immediate experience and given hidden meanings, symbols of the human condition and experience. Animals were ways to think, communicate and organise society, and it is this that we must endeavour to understand if we want to go beyond superficial appreciation of the art.

By far the most common animal depicted in Zimbabwean rock art was the kudu (*Tragelaphus strepsiceros*). The species is easily identified by their distinctive diamond-shaped ears twisted forward as in nature towards any noise or intrusion into their natural habitat. The males can be recognised by their thickset necks, the presence of mane (both often exaggerated in the art) and long,

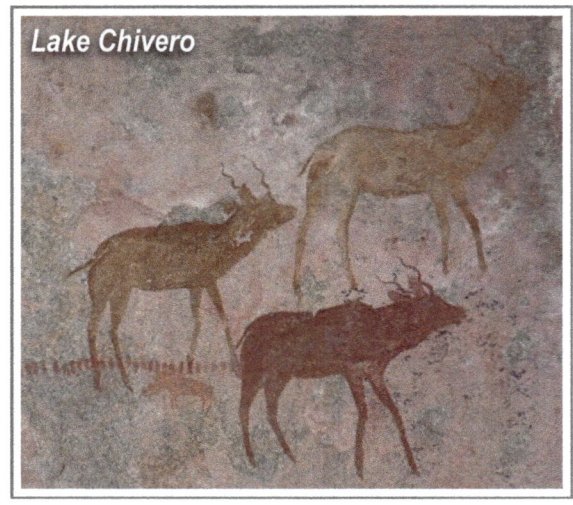
Lake Chivero

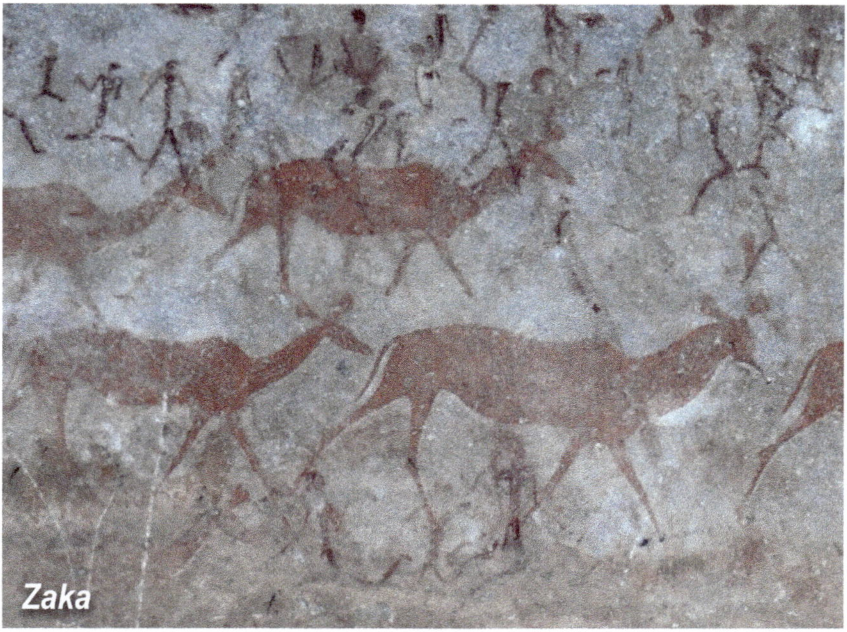

Zaka

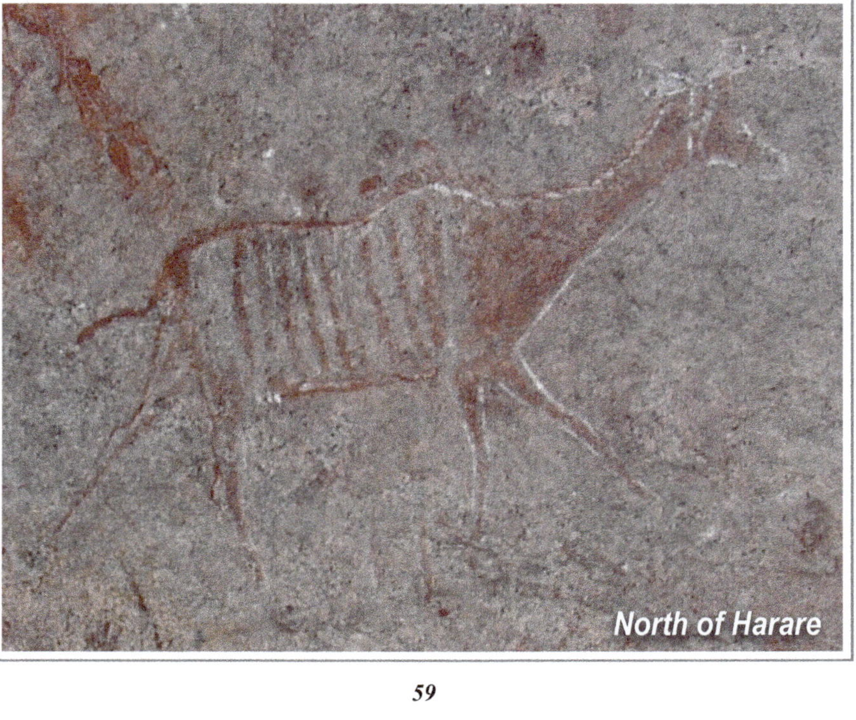

North of Harare

spiralling horns. Female kudu have curvy, elongated necks and no horns. Where present, you may be fortunate enough to see finer details, often painted in different colours - white outlines; the natural stripes on the flanks; colour accentuation on the inside of the ear and reproductive part; and other totally unnatural white lines across the leg joints and chest. These last resemble similar white lines on human figures. Thought to be bangle ornamentation, they transmute and fuse nature and humanity.

In Zimbabwe the kudu, a sociable antelope, seems to have been the prime symbol in the artists' symbolic repertoire. This is not only a reflection of our savanna woodland ecology, but expresses the perceived parallels which the community probably drew between the structures and behaviour of the kudu and their own society. The overt manliness of the male, bull kudu with its muscular form, exaggerated mane and obvious horns, contrasts with the more erotic curvilinear shape of the cows, female kudu. All of this in some way mirrors human gender stereotypes. Some authors have even suggested that through symbolic transformation the female kudu image was considered equivalent to the human woman.

However, it was not only in a matter of physical form that parallels may have been identified. The artist's depiction of a single or small groups of bull kudu (the bachelor herd) contrasts to the more frequent group images of the ever alert cows and juveniles (the breeding herd). This is not dissimilar to the gender-structured, economical divisions of Sān communities - the male hunter/s going about independently of the family group of gatherers. Furthermore, observed seasonal changes in kudu group size and composition were possibly equated to changing human patterns of dispersal and aggregation.

Less obvious to most modern observers is the fairly common portrayal of kudu breeding postures. Certain running and standing stances and facial expressions accompany kudu courtship. When in oestrus, kudu cows run with their necks stretched forward and slightly down, while the vulva is swollen and reddens. At this time the bull will come in hot-pursuit, drawn by the pheromones. Head raised, puckering his lips, panting and gasping, the male kudu chases down the object of his sexual desire. These themes are often seen in the art, they are literal elements of kudu behaviour which would have been observed and equated to human sexual behaviour. For this reason, the kudu seems to

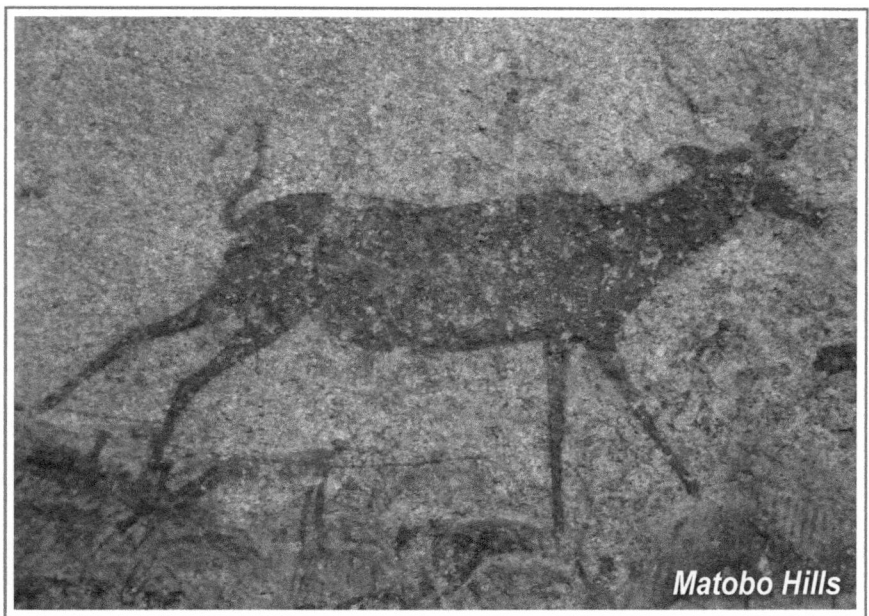
Matobo Hills

have been a powerful symbol painted in association with group depictions of Sān rites of passage - the need to shepherd and educate the neophyte girl on the occasion of her first bleed, and the adolescent boy's first hunt. In some instances, the animal paintings replaced entirely the human imagery.

For our Sān artists the kudu was a powerful, multifaceted symbol which dominated the painted composition, often making up at least 65% of all animal images. For the reasons discussed here, and probably many more unknown to us, the kudu was the animal of choice. It probably reminded the society of the gender divide in human economy and other social activity, as well as personal and social transformation giving entry into the society of adulthood; courtship and marriage; and with its hunting connections the kudu may be associated with human death. For the artists, the kudu was a principal way of thinking; it defined many elements of their society, a nexus of symbolism over and beyond being just a pretty picture.

While many other wild animals appear in our rock art, they are far less common than is the painted imagery of the kudu. This is not to say that these other species were socially unimportant, but the kudu appear to dominate our local symbolic code. In other regions, different species played a similar part: eland in uKhahlamba-Drakensberg mountains of South Africa/Lesotho and springbok in the dry interior of Namibia. What we are seeing is diversity in the social selection of symbols.

It is to these other, less frequently depicted species, that we now turn. They may not have been a central cultural theme as was the kudu, but each had its own symbolic meanings, expressing other animal/human associations. Sometimes they predominate at certain sites, expressing the site-specific activities, while there are also subtle regional variations. Sable and buffalo are more common in the rock art of northern Mashonaland, while giraffe are more noticeable in the art of the Matobo Hills and Limpopo Valley. This may reflect ecological differences as far as species preference, but social selection probably played a significant part.

It is important to understand that, as symbols, some animals were remembered and painted for their social meanings rather than existence. Other local animals were often neglected. For instance, in Zimbabwe eland (*Taurotragus oryx*) are rarely painted despite being historically present across the entire country. This contrasts with South Africa and Lesotho where depictions of the eland dominate most painted panels. There the eland played the same symbolic and ceremonial pivotal role for the Sān south of us as does the kudu north of the Limpopo River.

This is not to say that there are no paintings of eland in Zimbabwe. Where found, the depictions are often exquisite bi-chromes in gracious poses placed in prominent positions in larger caves, or completely dominate

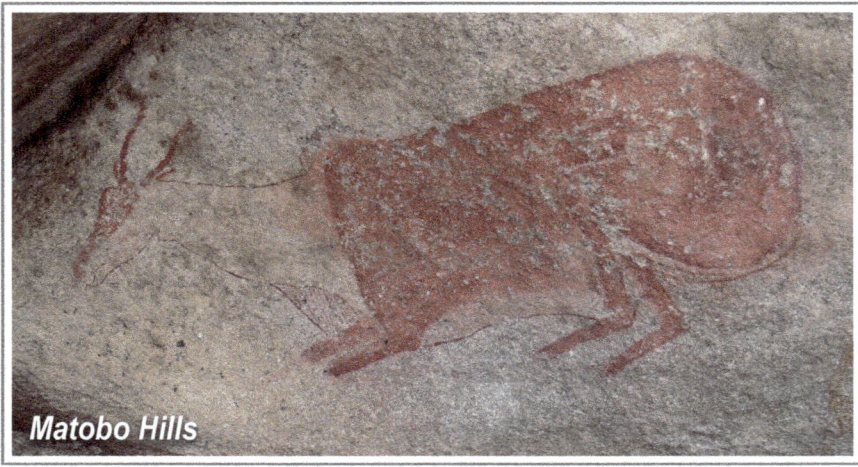

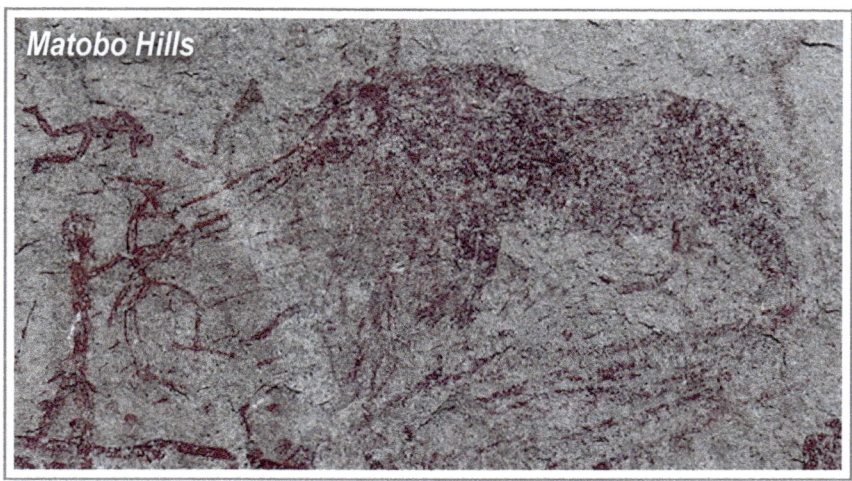

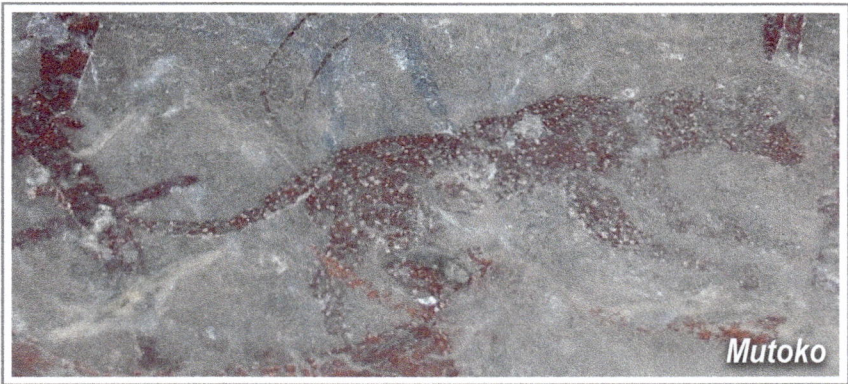

the animal depictions in smaller shelters. This massive meat and fat-rich herd animal must have had its own social significance. Great care was expended in painting it, but its symbolism must have been specific, not the all-embracing one of the Zimbabwe painted kudu. What this importance was, we find it particularly hard to say.

Paintings of felines are fairly common, although it is not always clear if they represent lion (*Panthera leo*), leopard (*Panthera pardus*) or cheetah (*Acinonyx jubatus*). In some instances it is just their characteristic footprints which denote the animal. The social habits of these large cats, clawed creatures, seem to have found no resonance in human society and most feline depictions appear as single creatures, generalised beasts of darkness, a danger and a threat to humanity. They would have featured as such, negative forces, in the stories told around the fireside. Many depictions show the animal attacking or being attacked by hunters. While these could be literal narratives of actual events, such encounters are often the talk of shamans after trance - encounters in the other world that they had with negative forces which had to be killed or driven off for the betterment of the community. It is likely that most of these feline hunting scenes were trance-related communication.

Although, as symbols, most feline depictions appear negative, sometimes the association was ambivalent. Modern Sān informants have told visiting ethnographers that at times powerful trancers would travel through the spirit world as felines, in so doing resolving human anxieties, doing good and not bad. From this it is clear that we cannot dismiss all feline images as unwholesome. The wider contexts of such depictions need to be carefully considered, what are they doing and with what other images were they painted.

Paintings of large dangerous animals, such as elephant (*Loxodonta africana*) and both species of rhinoceros (*Diceros bicornis* {black} and *Ceratotherium simum* {white}), often dominate the visual composition of many larger caves. Impressive there, as they are in the open veld, these paintings dominate the overall symbolic space.

Marching along either singularly or in family groups, many elephant images were crudely painted, consisting of an infill of smeared white clay. It has been suggested that the centrally located paintings of massive bull elephants, impressive beasts which wander the landscape seemingly

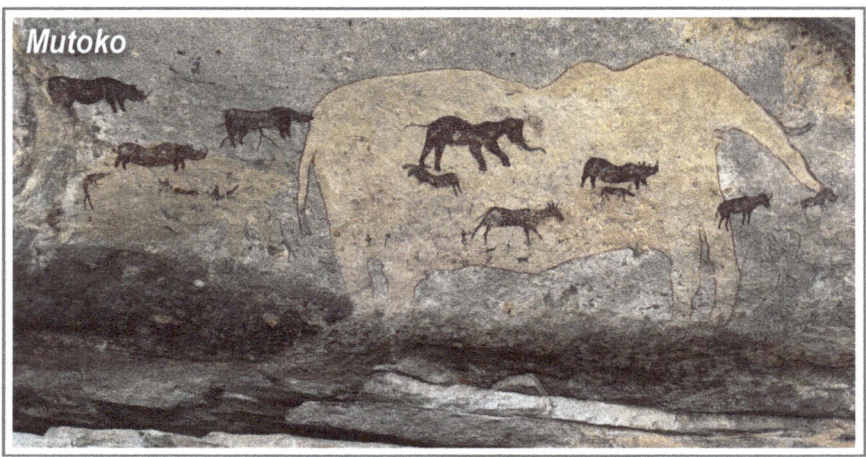

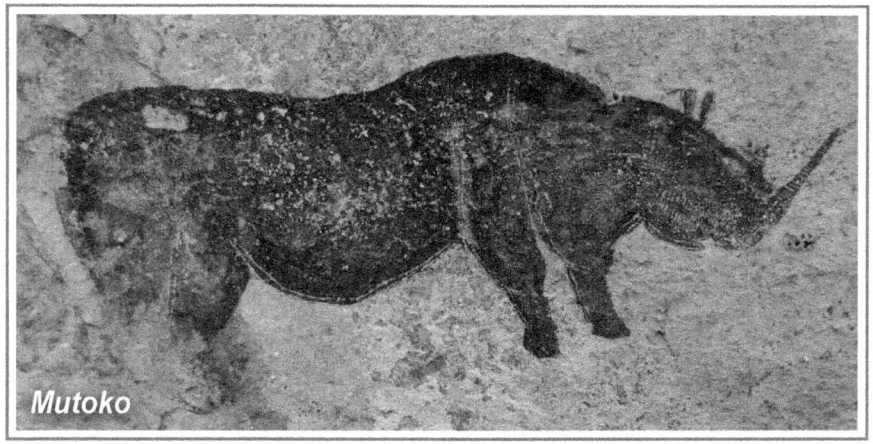
Mutoko

unfazed, were a favourite subject of myth, often tied to social categories. They may also have been a metaphor for the trancing shamans that likewise went forth during their spiritual work in the other realm. The close-knit structure of the maternal herds, which appear highlighted in other painted caves, often towards the sides, are suggestive of elephant symbolism more domestic, related to motherly concerns. In other instances, elephants appear as the focus of the metaphorical hunts, a painted composition already discussed [p.55)] As impressive in the rock art as in the natural world, the elephant was a powerful symbol with many different meanings, multilayered and contextual. In viewing and understanding the art it is necessary to take note of image's size, position, the herd structure and all associated images - all is not obvious.

The artists would have understood the contrasting social habits and tempers of the black and the white rhinoceros. In the art, while somewhat difficult to separate due to artistic stylisation, it seems that many (if not most) rhinoceros depicted in Zimbabwean rock art are black rhinoceros. A browser, they are usually solitary, potentially aggressive creatures. As such, they were probably branded in the communities' stories as an undesirable, bad and destructive spirit. It has been suggested that these images may also represent the angry shaman who brings misfortune and division in the community, as well as "he-rain" - violent and destructive storms accompanied by lightening and strong winds of temper. As such, these shaman, through the symbolism of these animals, were to be driven away or symbolically killed in the realm of the trance ceremony. The presence of small white

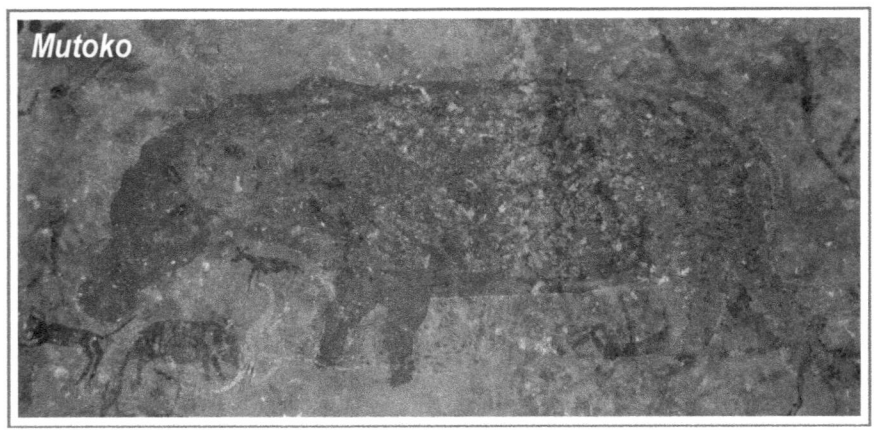
Mutoko

dots and lines on some painted rhinoceros, recasts the wild animal into the realm of humans; it is a transformed human.

Not surprisingly, the unusual habits of the hippopotamus (*Hippopotamus amphibius*) attracted the symbolic interest of the artists. Occupying two spheres of reality, water and land, it was an animal of ambivalence, neither one nor the other, and as such was thought to have significant but dangerous magical powers. The hippo had considerable *n/om,* divine power. It was often associated with rain and the renewal that comes from rain falling on the dry African landscape. The now extinct /Xam community of the parched Northern Cape knew it as *!Khwa-ka-xoro,* the rain cow, which was so important in their mythology and ceremonies. In the other world around them, accessed by way of trance ceremonies, the spirit hippo was said to be captured and dragged over the landscape to be figuratively killed, thereby bringing about rain. In our own rock art, we should not interpret the apparent "hippo hunts" as literal, but as representing the constant processes of environmental and social change/renewal/seasonality, as well as the positive outcomes of the trance dance.

Paintings of sable (*Hippotragus niger*), zebra (*Equus quagga burchellii*) and giraffe (G*iraffa camelopardalis*) appear throughout the country, although with some regional preferences. They are generally carefully painted, sometimes using two or more colours. The white/black stripes on the bodies of the first two and the network of patches on the giraffe are painted with special care, indicating that they had very special meanings to the artists. Some authors believe that these species represent the gynocentric element of society, feminine grace embodied in their

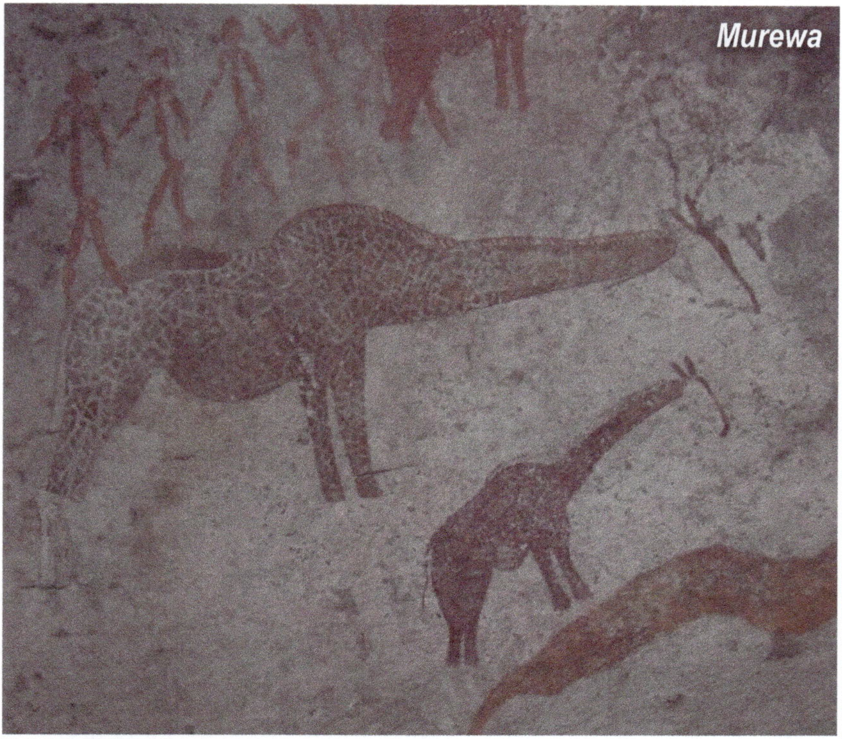

Murewa

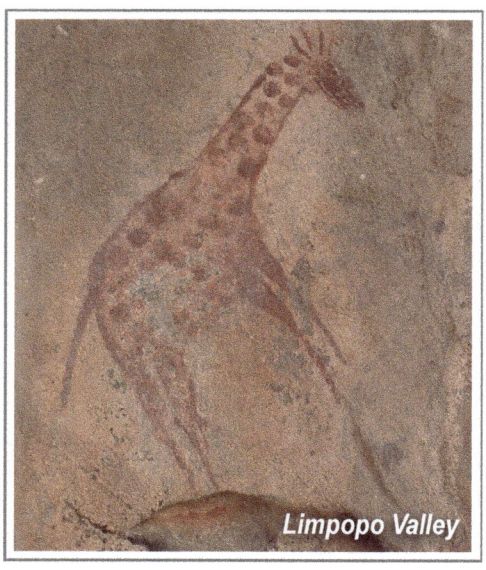

Limpopo Valley

movements and beauty. The zebra, always apparently fat and healthy, with its curvaceous stripes, is described by some Sān groups as actually being a woman; the animal is effectively genderised and symbolically redefined into the human realm where it was used as a symbol in stories, ceremonies and in the art. But this is not the only cultural association carried by these animals. Just like young and pregnant women, these species are said

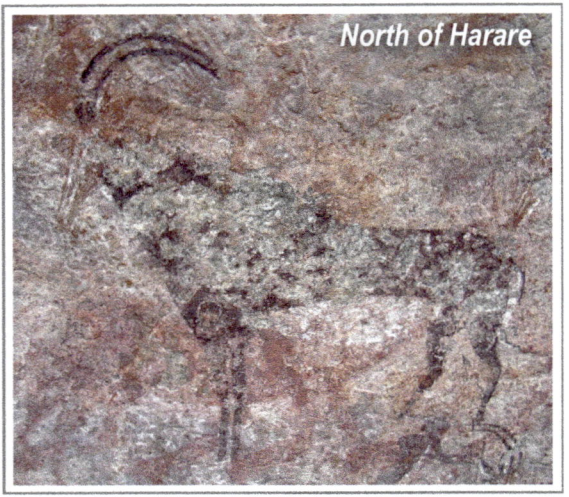
North of Harare

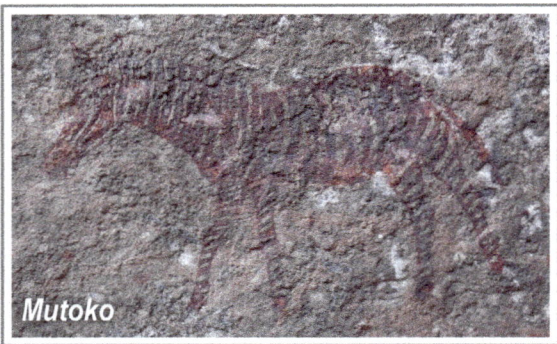
Mutoko

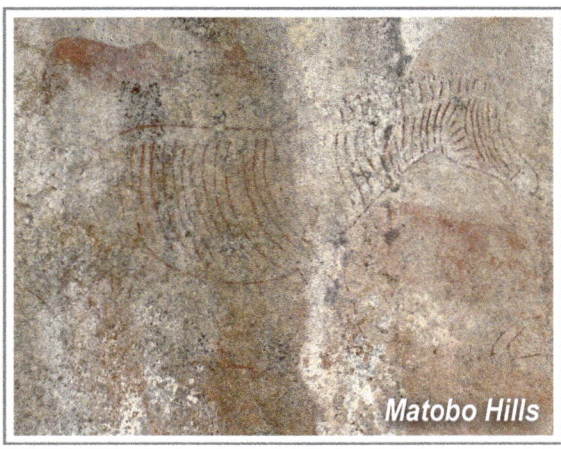
Matobo Hills

to have plentiful divine power, *n/om,* that is said to bring about rain, and in consequence environmental and social well being. They are therefore often called upon to empower the shamans through the singing of their respective songs during the trance dance, as well as being celebrated in other Sān ceremonies. Their depiction is more than a mere picture.

In contrast, buffalo (*Syncerus caffer*) and tsessebe (*Damaliscus lunatus*) may have been male, androcentric, human symbols, existing in binary opposition to the three species discussed above. Through size and display, the bulls of these species protect their herds, something that may have been equated by these people to the communities and their territories, *n!oresi.* Given that many of the tsessebe are shown standing in a rigid, upright position, a

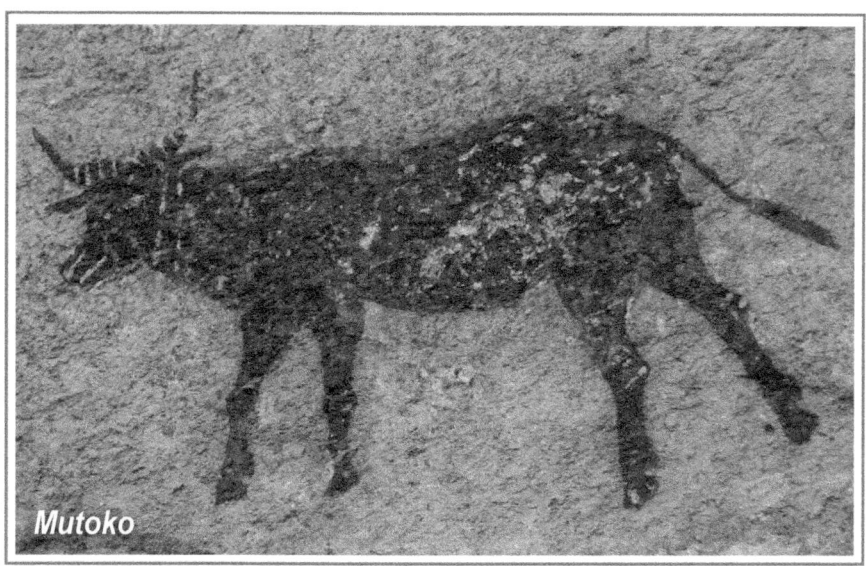

posture adopted by the resident territorial males during courtship, suggests a symbolic association with courtship and marriage.

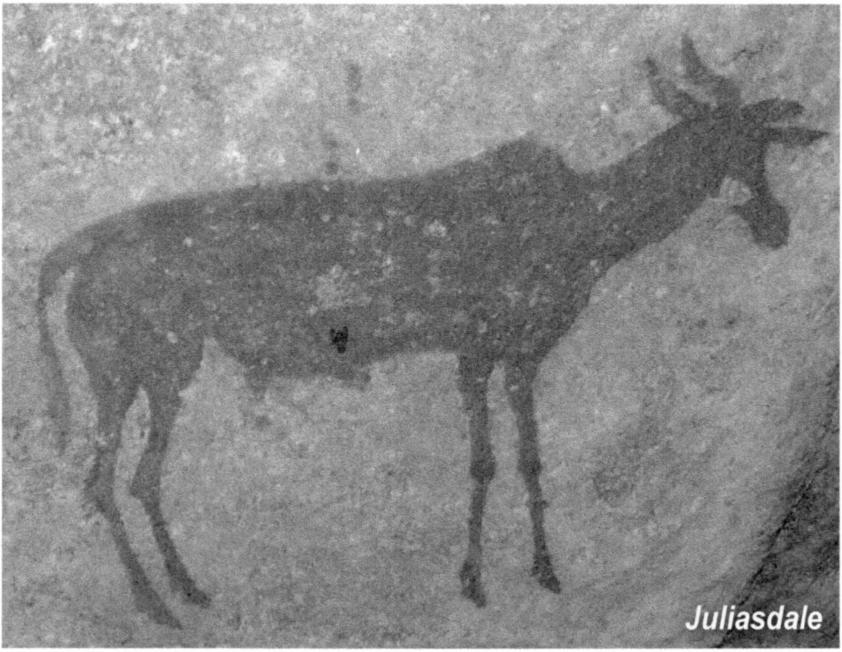

Smaller antelope were less frequently depicted, despite the fact that they constituted an important part of the community's meat diet. They are also rarely identifiable to species. In part this may be because we, in our lack of experience, are unable to identify them. Or there may have been intentional obscurity; these animals being stylised and without persona similar to the artists' conventional portrayal of the human figures.

Interestingly, blue wildebeest (*Connochaetes taurinus*) were infrequently depicted. Despite being herd animals suitable for human symbolism, they are seemingly overlooked. Possibly this is because the wildebeest is highly skittish, its alarm calls and antics prompting other animals to flight. Some Sān stories suggest that the wildebeest were once people. Aggrieved with their current forsaken place in world, they undermine the hunt, scaring away the game as an act of revenge. Because of this, the wildebeest seems to have been avoided as symbolic capital. Those depictions which are known, need to be considered in relation to the other images/symbols with which they are painted.

A surprising depiction are aardvark (*Orycteropus afer*). A nocturnal creature rarely seen, its burrows are a conspicuous feature in the African bush. Many communities believe that aardvarks, African antbears, are spiritually powerful creatures. Their body parts are said to

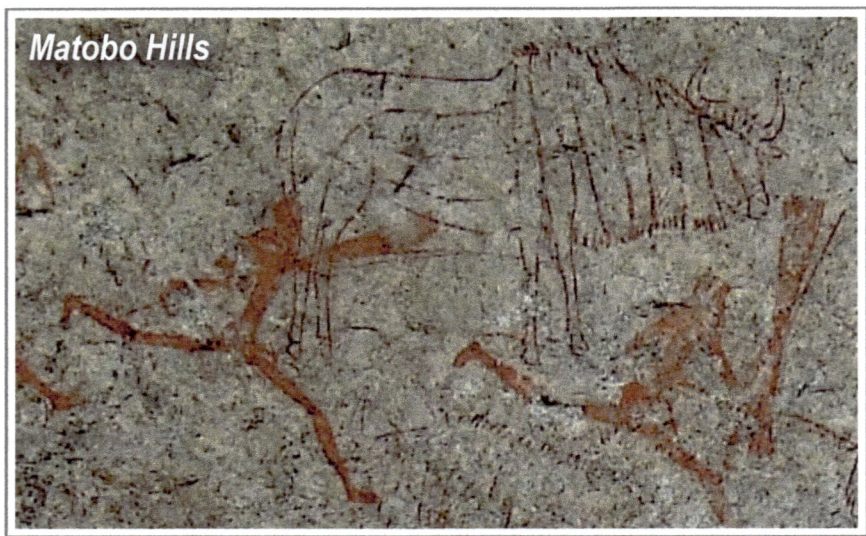

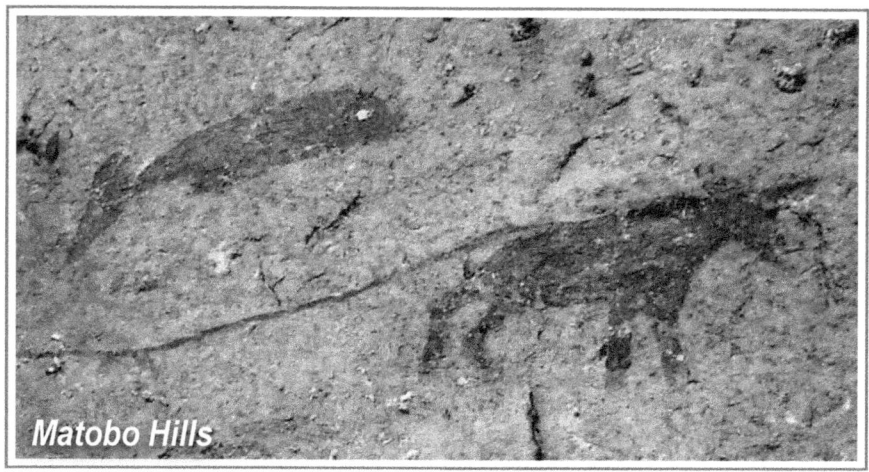

confer magical properties on their owners, so warding off evil spirits and physical threat. The animal's copious body fat; pig-like snout; human-like feet; its ever-active pursuit of insects, most especially termites [pp 86-87]; and its burrowing habits, render the aardvark as an animal of extreme ambivalence, failing to fit standards of definition. It was both feared and admired. The Sān believed that the aardvark possesses tremendous divine power which is drawn upon in many ceremonies. The shaman and the aardvark are said to become one at the height of the trance dance - there is a common experience of darkness, of being underground and of bodily ambiguity.

Some Sān myths associate the aardvark with the social role of women. It is said that a female aardvark assigned the different ecological niches to various animals, thereby bringing about harmony and order in the natural world. In a similar vein, Sān women distil order out of the potential

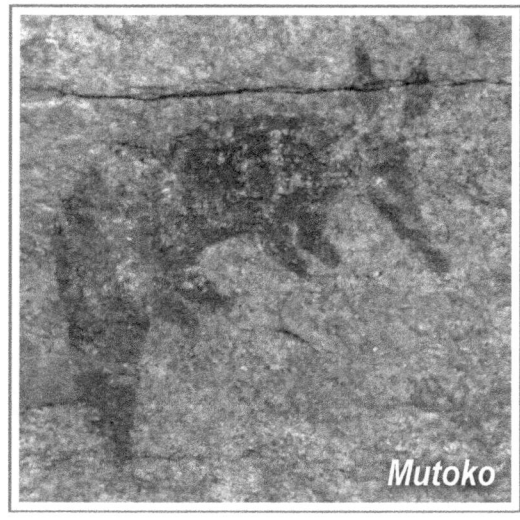

71

social chaos of community living. In ceremonies and as painted symbols, the aardvark and human women may have been considered one and the same, powerful, desirable and capable of dispelling disorder.

Baboons (*Papio ursinus*) were regularly depicted in the art, although interestingly, not the other smaller primates. Elements of the artists' own society would have found resonance with that of the baboon troop as far as age and "authority"; gender roles; communication; and foraging strategies are concerned. It is often said that the baboons are another people beloved by the creator before being displaced in his affection by humans and driven into the wilderness. In consequence, antagonistic to all humans, the baboons are said to thwart human gathering and hunting strategies, rendering hunting grounds barren.

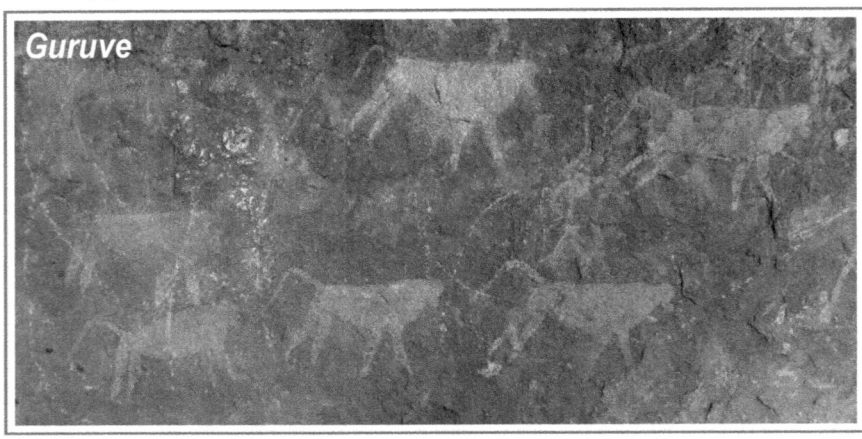

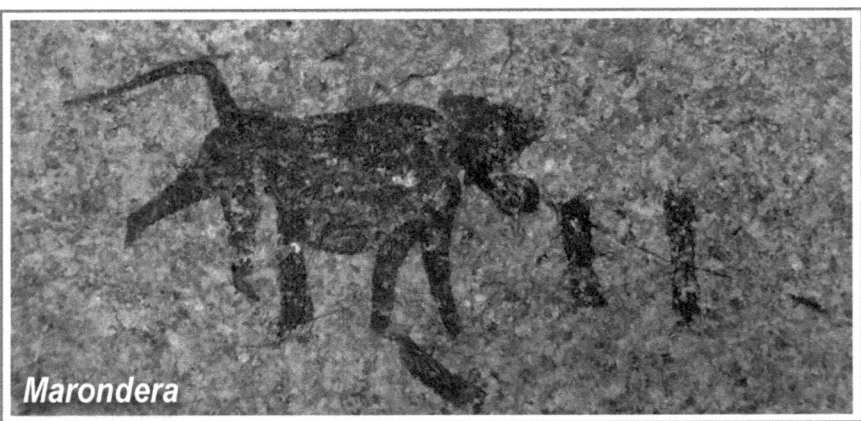

Lying on the cusp of what was defined as human, baboons were yet another powerful symbol of ambivalence. Being neither human nor wild animals they were both respected and despised. Their inclusion in the rock art would have been complex, probably with multiple meanings depending on the context - as a positive kindred people with social structure; as a negative force tied to anti-social behaviour; as a source to sacred powers called upon at times of social and physical uncertainty (rites of passage). In addition, the lone wanderings of the old dog baboon apart from the troop, would also have found resonance in the activities of the human hunter or shaman.

Depictions of reptiles were rare, with the exception of crocodiles and snake-like forms. The crocodile (*Crocodylus niloticus*) was a regular symbolic theme. Another animal of ambivalence, it is found on both land and in water, able to move (transition) between both. A dangerous reptile, it appears docile while basking on the sandbanks, but threatens unseen death when lurking in the watery pools. It lays eggs like a bird, but has the scales of a reptile. In all of this, the crocodile defies easy

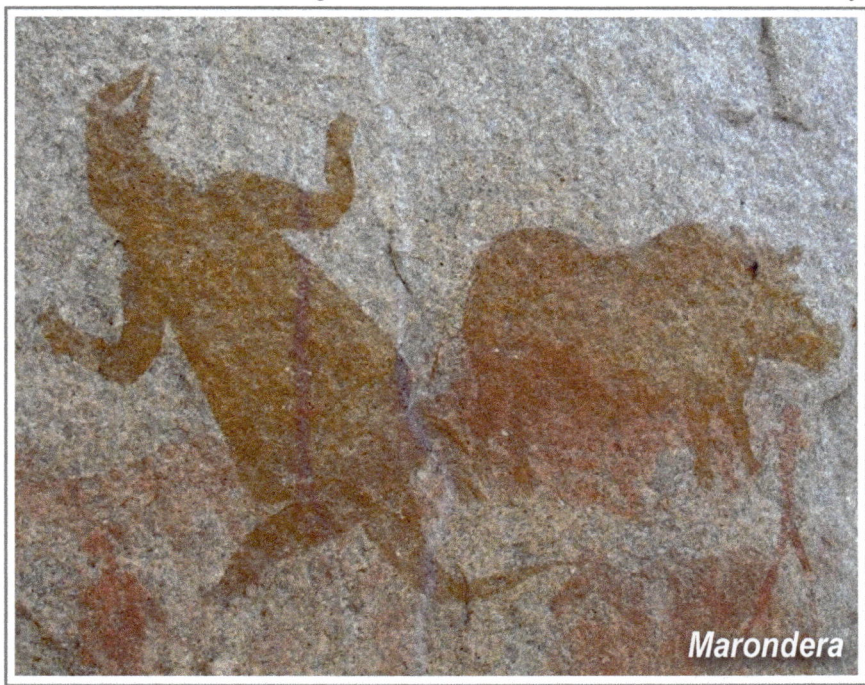

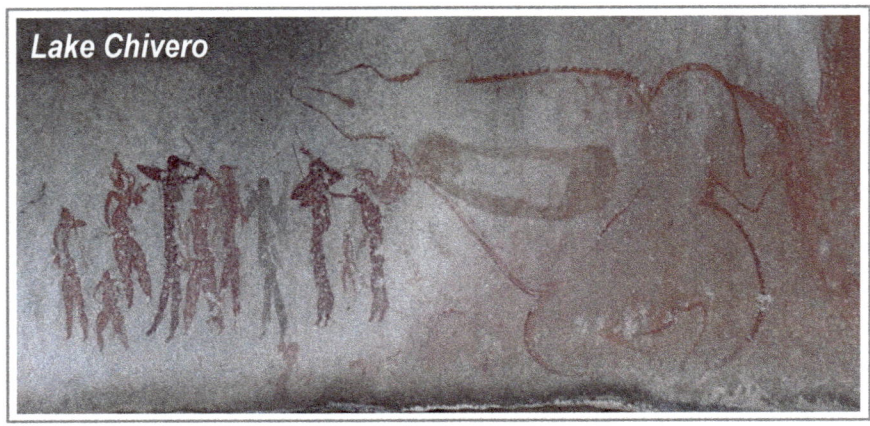
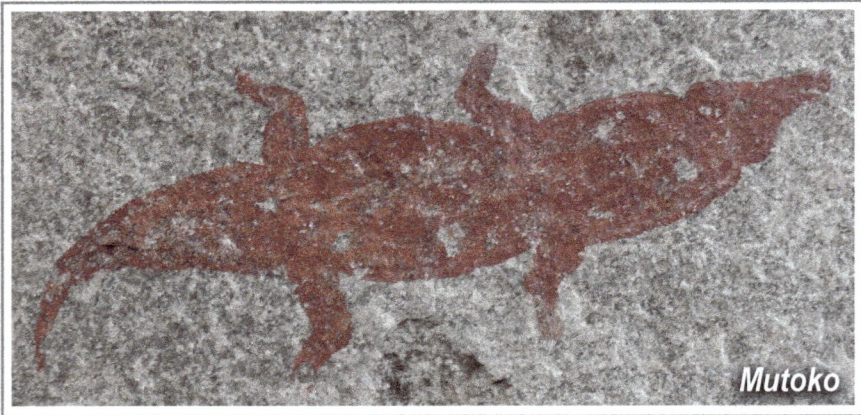

categorisation. It fits no predefined human category. It is therefore not surprising that crocodile imagery, its scales and its body fat, are traditionally esteemed as powerful medicines, and for many African societies the crocodile is a multifaceted symbol, associated with danger, death, male virility, procreation and rainfall.

As a painted symbol and in their stories, the Sān artists probably held many similar views. In its ambivalence, the crocodile was a power force to be called upon at times of transition, rites of passage, as well as being a source of power for shaman who "die" in the trance dance ceremonies. It has been suggested that some shaman become crocodiles as they "sink into the waters" of deeper hallucination. The art is neither literal, nor with only one rendering. One needs to look for context, associations in the complex painted panel.

Most snake-like paintings cannot be assigned to any one species and it appears that symbolically they were combined as one simplified form. Much like the human figures in our art, it was the essence of the snake that was important, not its specific details. Often snake-like forms seem to writhe across the rock face, the spiritual interface between this world and that beyond/inside the rock. In some cases, they were painted as if entering or leaving natural rock cracks or holes, sacred portals in the rock face. In some caves the heads of massive, snake-like

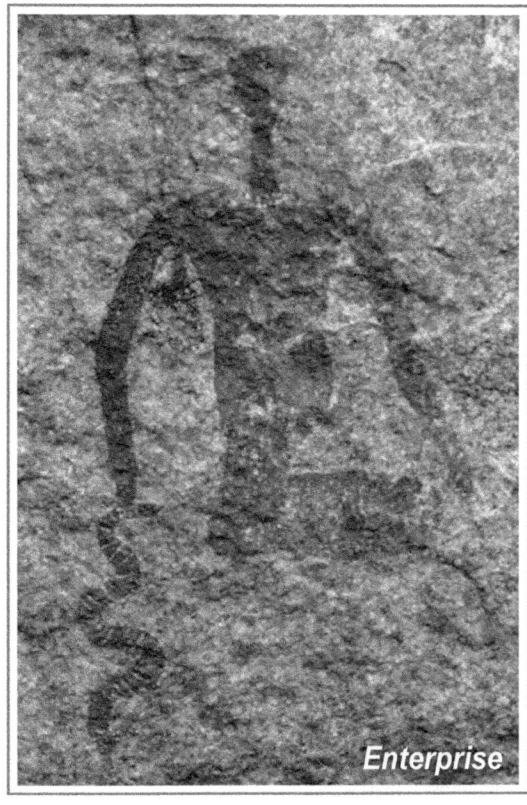
Enterprise

depictions are painted at points of the most notable echo; an interplay between art, acoustics and a perceived cosmic pathway to the divine.

Snakes are particularly ambivalent creatures. Feared because they are potentially dangerous, they move without legs or wings. They traverse the three principal realms of existence - water, land and air. Snakes are symbols of transition, creatures of all worlds and messengers of the divine, to say nothing of their more obvious sexual innuendoes. They were symbols exploited in a multitude of ceremonial activities and mythology. Shaman, for instance, may be likened to snakes as they metaphorically move while in trance, sometimes deriving their power from the creature. This association may account for the fairly common depiction in the Mashonaland East and Nyanga districts of people holding and sitting or dancing amongst snakes.

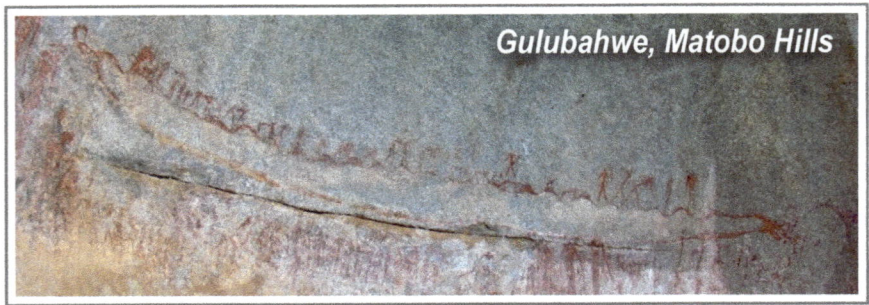
Gulubahwe, Matobo Hills

Some snake-like paintings combine the sinuous body with features of humans and other animals. This fusion of spiritual powers strengthens the image's symbolic capital. The integration of the specified features of dangerous animals, such as the tail of the scorpion or the teeth of the crocodile, together with the acoustic alertness of the kudus' ears, combines the divine powers and social meanings into one. This is often strengthened further through the addition of other figures walking along or touching the "snake" - trancing human figures, hunters, therianthropic forms, other wild animals of *n/om*.

In several instances, snake-like creatures dominate a particular painted cave. Such places probably had specific geographically discreet ceremonial functions in which this powerful imagery played a key part - the rituals gave rise to the images painted, which in turn determined the nature of the ceremonies conducted at such sites. For instance, some authors have described the massive snake of Gulubahwe Cave in the eastern Matobo Hills as mythical, a parable about the creation and unity of life in the "hills". But it would have been more than a simple story. The very presence of this image would have both resulted from, and thereafter determined, the social activities associated with this location.

Occasionally we find depictions of fish in the rock art, although never common. While fish may have been a regular source of food, this was not the reason they were painted. Most fish paintings are found some distance from suitable water bodies, while not all species were depicted. Most images belong to the Mormyrid species. These fish are known for their unusual electrogenic properties; they are fish which will give you a zap. This unusual property would have been known by the artists who selectively depicted the species for this very reason. Ethnographic accounts suggest that the sharp, unexpected tingling feeling is akin to the experiences of pain felt by the shaman during the trance dance ceremony.

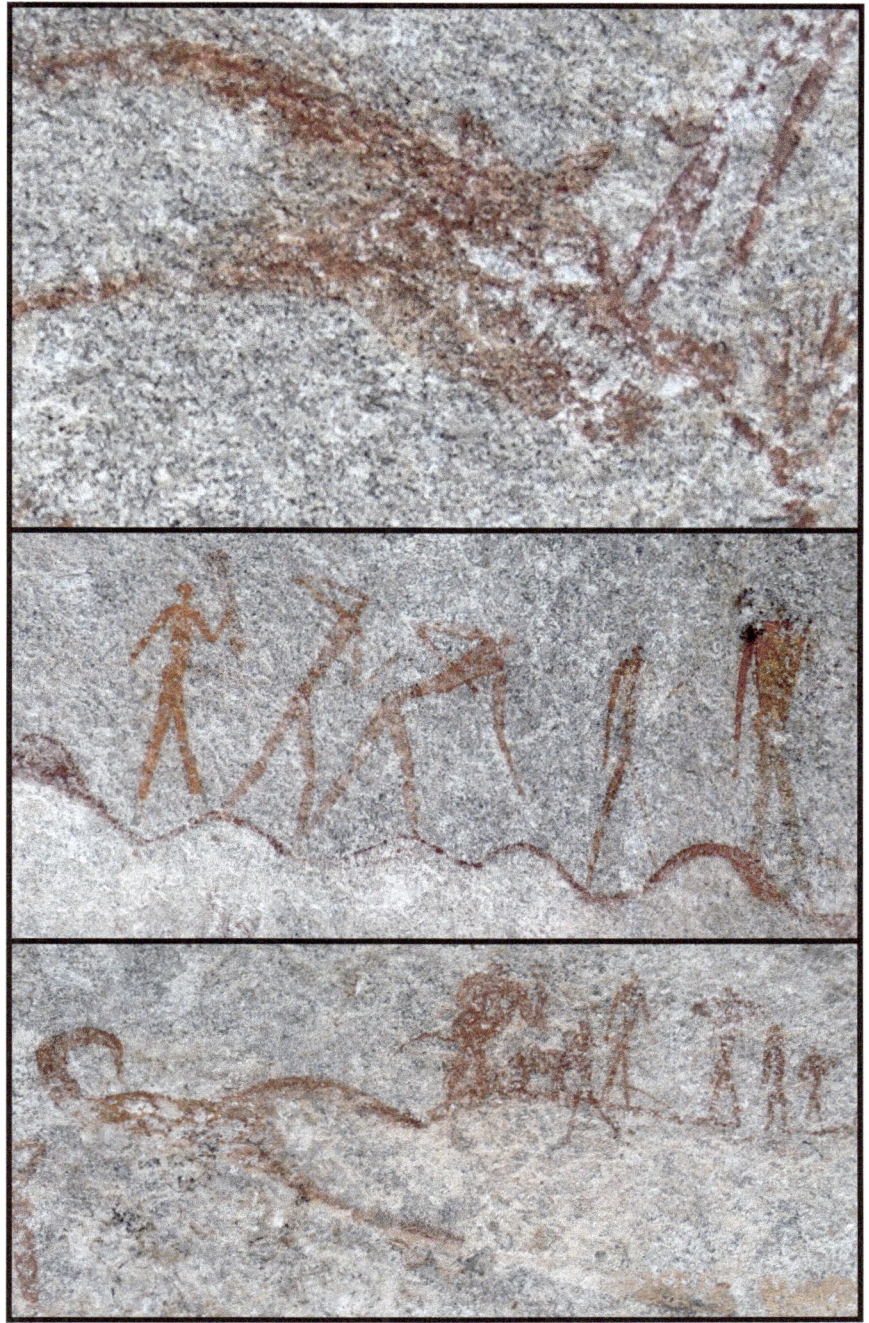

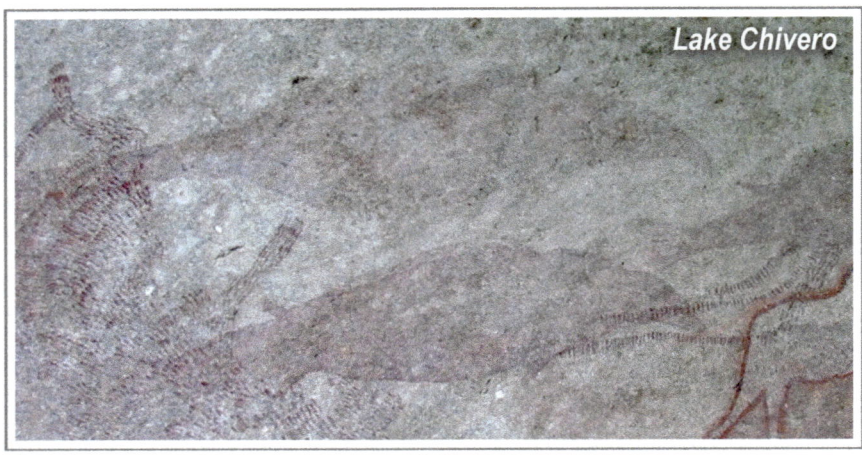

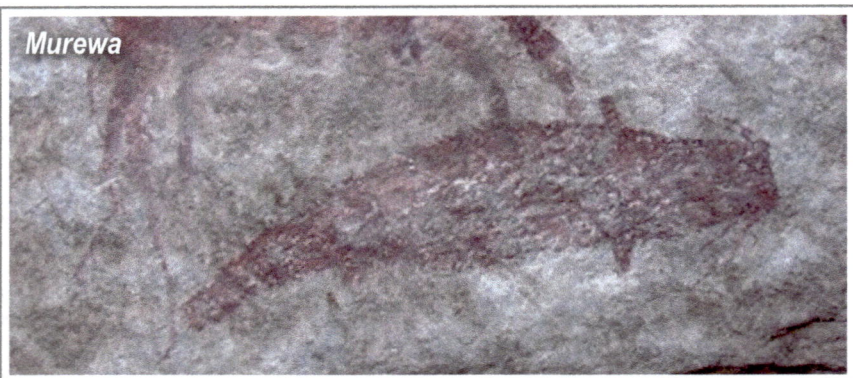

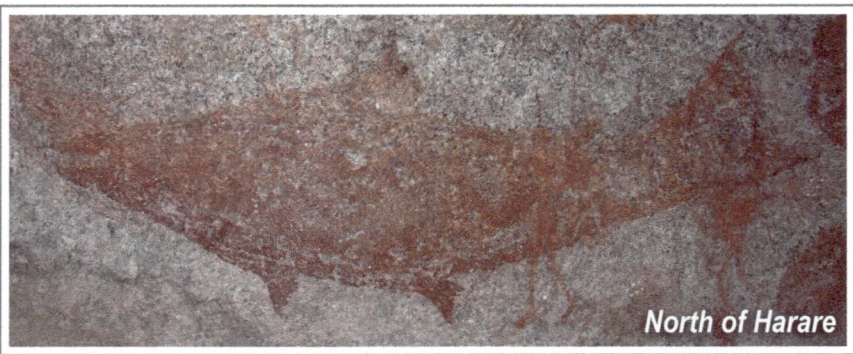

Where painted, the incorporation of these fish images transform what may seem an obvious group scene into one in the world beyond, in the realm of the spirits, of stories and the works of shamans.

Barbel (*Clarias gariepinus*) are occasionally painted. Lung fish, which can, at a push, migrate across land and burrow deep into the muds to survive drought conditions, are anomalous and would have attracted symbolic capital. In some instances, tiger fish (*Hydrocynus vittatus*) are shown, probably symbolic representations which make reference to aggression, and the human emotions and fears that go with this. Ambiguous in the category of fish, the tigerfish may have been the riverine equivalent to the feline imagery already discussed.

Paintings of birds were infrequent. Often eaten, the consumption of game birds, with the exception of the ostrich, was limited to the family unit and were not hunted meat shared across the wider community. As such, birds were not generally deemed "useful in thought".

The exceptions generally depict specific species of birds and bird-like creatures which would have been subject to stories and myth, as well as being associated with certain ceremonial settings, more especially the transformation of body and spirit in the trance dance ceremony. The ability of birds to fly, to leave the confines of the ground, would have been a useful metaphor for the shaman experiencing out of body travel, flying through the air. In the Matobo Hills there is a unique painting of what appears to be a trancing shaman or spirit figure holding onto streaming lines behind a massive eagle or vulture.

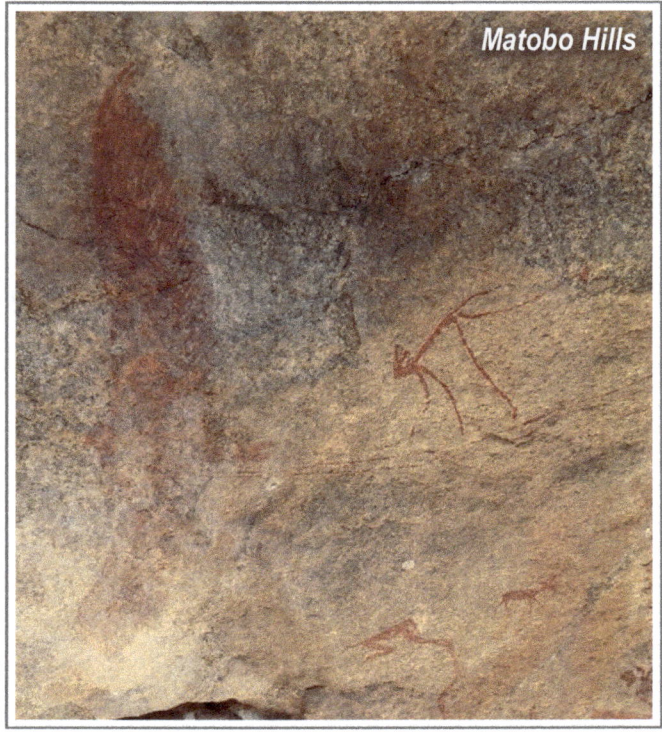

Matobo Hills

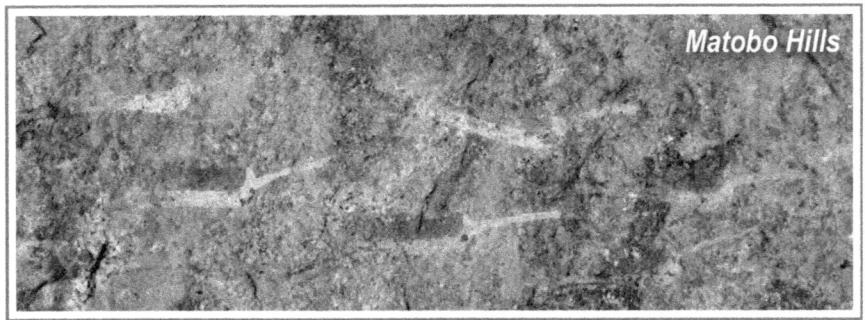
Matobo Hills

The presence at other painted sites of therianthropic birds, often in various stages of transformation between bird and human and antelope, seems to support this shamanistic interpretation, or they may have been creatures of mythology or stories of the multifaceted spirits which exist in the world around us. A feature not often noted when looking at the art is that the legs of many painted bird images are reversed, suggesting that they are human images and not avian.

In some caves, swallows and migratory storks were painted. Both these avian species arrive with the pending seasonal rains and were symbols of renewal, probably in some way associated with rain-making ceremonies. Ostrich and small game birds, more especially guineafowl, would have had their own meanings, they were more than mere food. The inability of the former to fly marks it out as yet another creature of ambivalence, a creature of divine power. On the other hand, the seasonal changes in guineafowls' behaviour from dispersal in the wet/breeding season to their combining as large flocks in the dry, post-breeding season, may have found symbolic resonance with the artists whose own society had similar cycles of aggregation and dispersal. The bird was more than mere food for the stomach, it was also food for human thought.

Insects are generally absent from the art, although they would have been gathered and eaten. An exception not usually recognised are "flying ants", the reproductive stage of the termite colony when flying male and female *alates* emerge from their nests to mate and form colonies elsewhere. In a few instances, we have clear paintings of termites, depicted individually or as swarms, but more often they are shown as an abstract concept, speckles and formlings [pp 96-98]. Here suffice to say that these creatures were important symbols selected because of their flight; their association with the rains; their fat (a desirable food generally scarce in the African veld); and their apparent

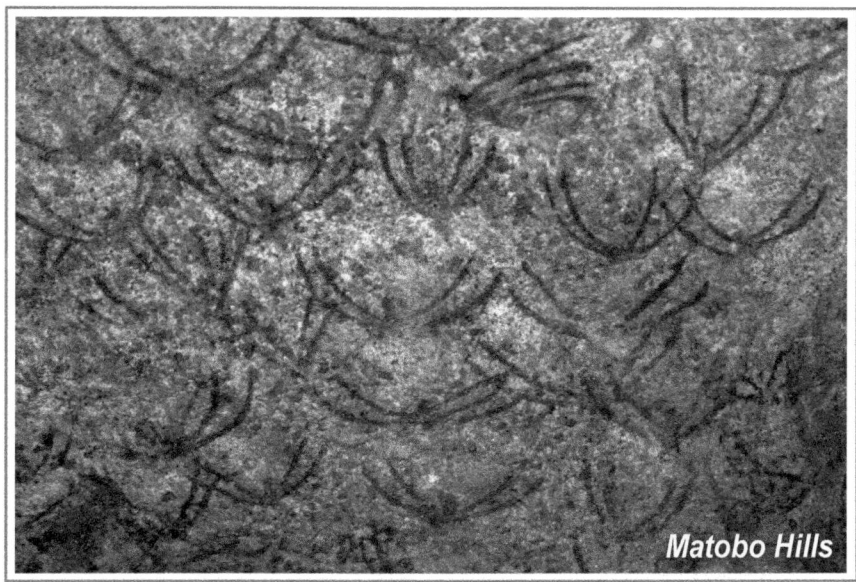
Matobo Hills

interface from the ground through to the sky. All these literal associations would have resonated with the experiences of the shaman and the concept of natural divine power, *n/om*, that exists in the everyday world of Sān communities, now and in the past. The concepts of environmental well-being and transition in rites of passage were all symbolically embodied in these small, often overlooked creatures which feature in our art.

Other animals can be found in Zimbabwe's diverse rock art, our coverage is not exhaustive. What were the symbolic meanings behind the portrayal of dog (both wild & domestic), jackal, lizard, mongoose, porcupine, reedbuck, warthog, bushpig, domestic stock (goats & cattle) and many others? There is much which requires further investigation as far as both ethnographical and animal behavioural studies. The art is complex, drawing on multiple facets of the literal and the socially-determined symbolic associations based upon these. We have spent some time considering the animal forms which appear in our rock art, not because this is a scrapbook of wildlife paintings, but because the painted animals, no less than the painted human forms, were a complex code of socially significant meanings to the Sān artists. They encapsulated human qualities and definitions including gender, age, emotions, sexual activity, bodily and ceremonial transformation and an artistic expression of a human understanding of the cosmology.

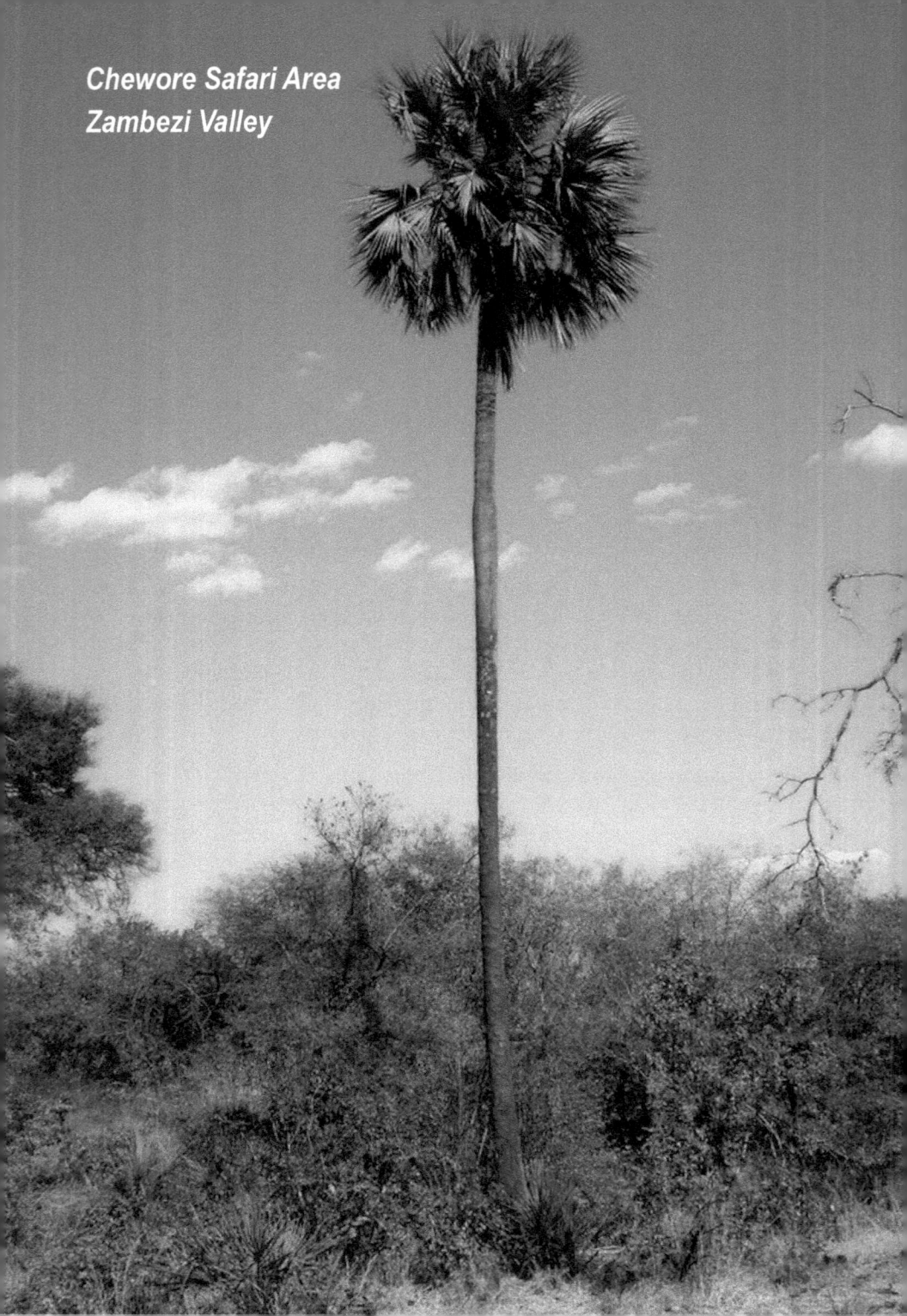

Plants and the Cosmos

Depictions of plants are uncommon, consisting mostly of images of plant bulbs and occasionally trees. Unlike the realm of animals, it is as if plants were not really conceived of as the subject matter of symbols. This is in marked contrast to the deep Sān knowledge of plants as food, medicines, and as raw materials for shelter and manufacture of tools. The point is that the artists did not think symbolically of plants to the same extent as they did animals.

The tree-like images which occur were generally highly stylised and it is difficult to assign them to any one species. Possible exceptions are the occasional palm trees, the depictions of which are sometimes found a long way from where they grow naturally. Indeed, many of the tree-like depictions may in fact be highly stylised derivatives of the palm, the essence of the plant rather than botanical details being considered important.

It has been suggested by Siyakha Mguni that the palm, an "unusual" tree, ambiguous in classification, was symbolically representative of the Sān view of the cosmos. Slow in growth, with deep and widespread roots, and a tall unbranched trunk with an uppermost cluster of leaves, he argues that they viewed the palm as a physical manifestation of the abstract links, the life force, that traversed between the conceptual spheres of earth, sky and water, the human campsite and the remote wilderness of the landscape. It was a symbolic link, a pathway to the divine, the creator and the spiritual realm in the sky and the other world beyond - a link to "god's house".

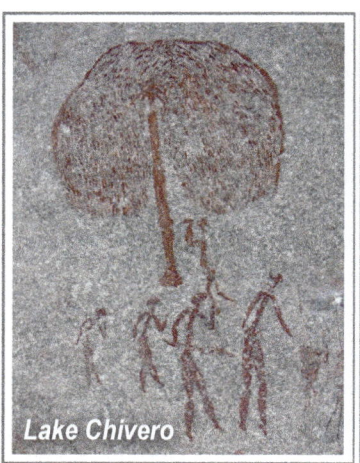
Lake Chivero

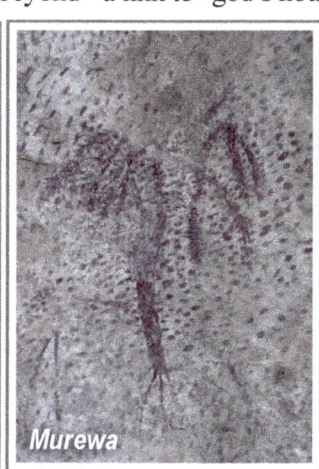
Murewa

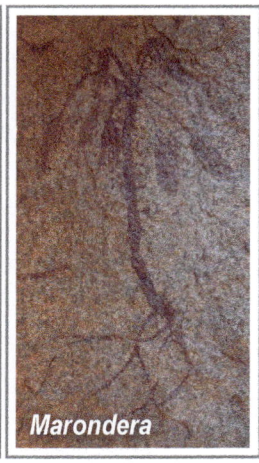
Marondera

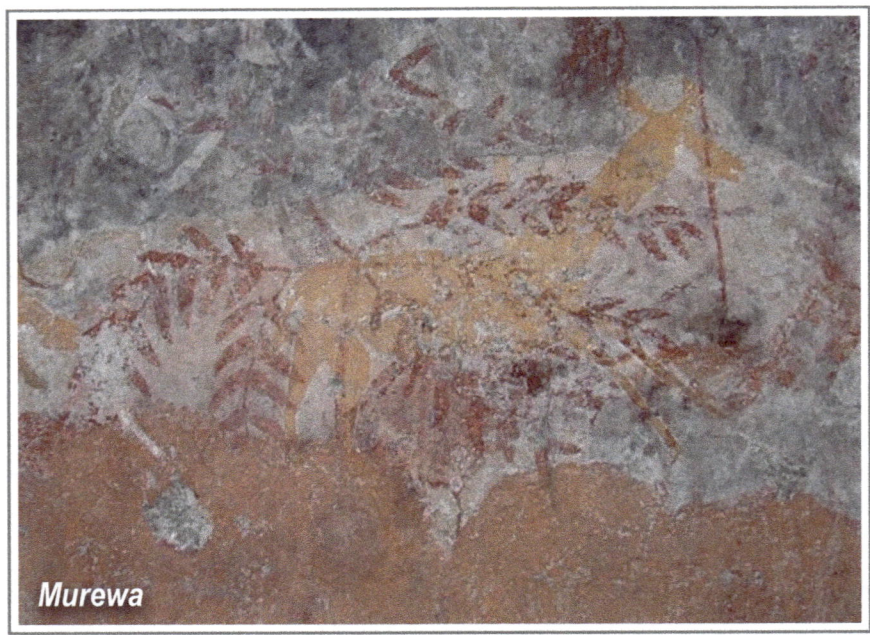
Murewa

This association of spirituality and the divine power embodied by these tree-like images was heightened through its painted connection with other symbolically charged objects - flecks, termites, *n/om,* human shaman figures and their animal equivalents. As such, the palm/tree, a literal point of reference in the world around them, was transformed into an object of cosmic explanation, and a figurative route to the world beyond, one which could be exploited in ceremonies and by trancing shaman.

Other painted tree-like images are more difficult to identify, let alone explain. Some may represent musasa (*Brachystegia spiciformis*) whose striking changing of colours from orange and red to green still enchant a modern observer each and every spring. Was this transition recognised and tied symbolically by the artists' society - rites of passage, seasonal environmental renewal and the expression of hopes for rains in the coming summer season? Once again we should not look for the obvious in the art, the western scientific literal, but we must seek the deeper meanings.

Slightly more common in the art are various bulb-like forms, although they are equally difficult to understand. On a literal level, they may relate to some of the basic plant foods collected by women. Not only reservoirs of water and food, some bulbs hold medical and hallucinatory properties.

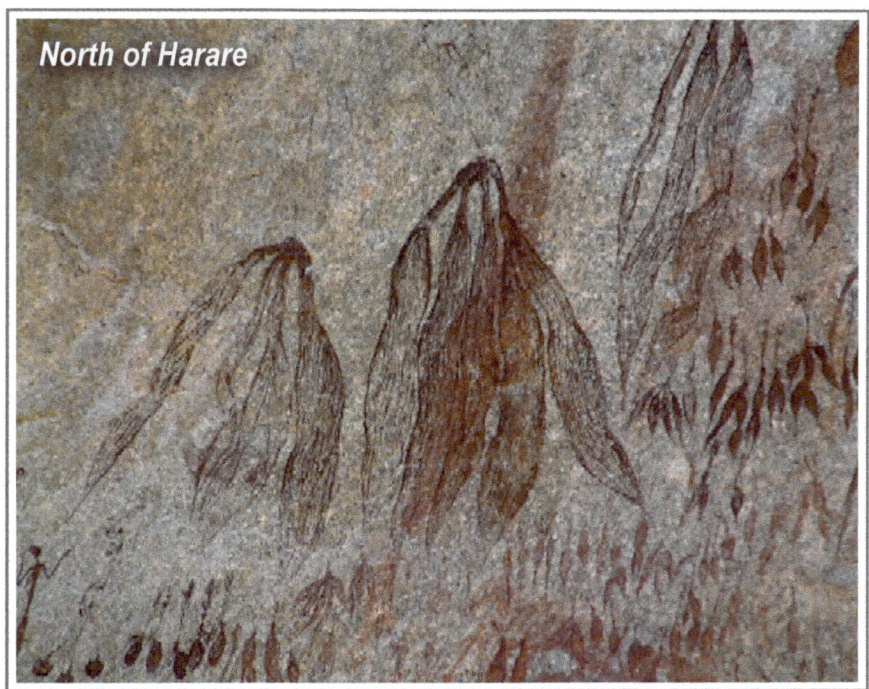

North of Harare

Their depiction may be a gynocentric symbol, proclaiming the otherwise understated foraging activities of women and may even be symbols expressed in female rites of passage. Shelters, where these images dominate the painted composition, may have been woman's places; space set aside for particular female ceremonial activities.

There have been some suggestions that some of these painted bulbs were hallucinatory, capable of inducing altered states of consciousness exploited by shaman. However, there is little evidence in Sān ethnography for the use of plant-based hallucinatory drugs. Instead it is the trance dance, the bigger inclusive communal activity, that was culturally important. The use of drugs is a far more individualistic affair, unlikely to be a Sān social activity.

The whole issue of plant depictions requires a lot more research. As with animal symbolism, we must seek the symbolic meanings which have literal points of referral - things that the people knew and aspects which were selected and transformed to capture a non-literal human association.

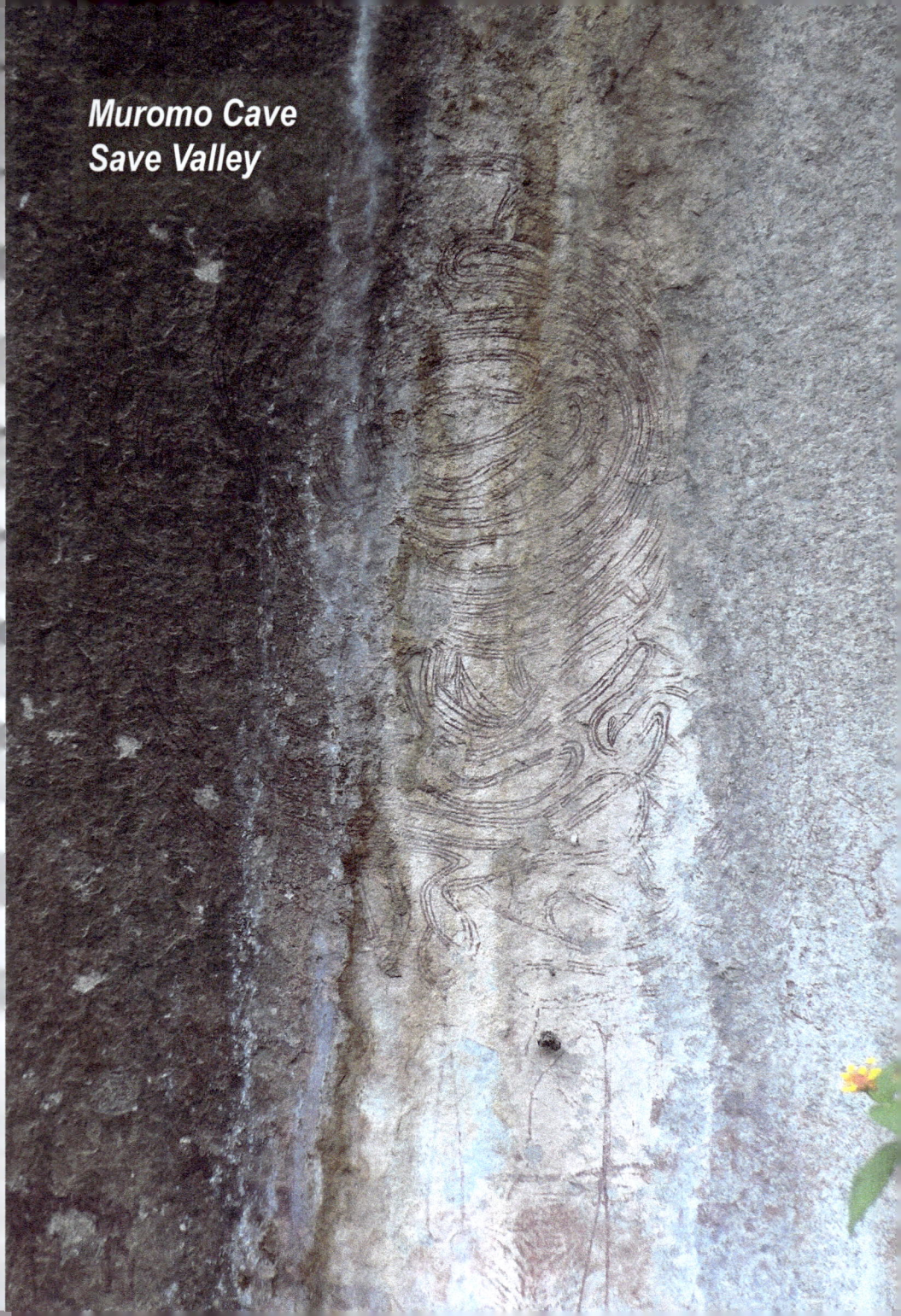

*Muromo Cave
Save Valley*

Abstract Images of Association

Not all of the depictions found in our rock art have a basis in reality. Some images may have been entirely mythical, creatures of the imagination told in stories of legend. Possibly this includes those paintings of strange "animals"; huge antelope-headed snakes or bird-headed hippopotamus-like creatures. For the Sān the western separation of fact, myth, and their explanation of the cosmos did not apply; all were multifaceted aspects of their rationalisation of the divine in the past, the present and the future.

There are also abstract paintings, images which have, to our eyes at least, no literal point of referral. This includes many painted lines of dots and dashes. Undulating across the rock face, they often appear to link diverse images, unifying them into a single composition. The late Peter Garlake believed them to be entirely metaphysical, representing the flowing movements of divine power and the very energy of life across the ceremonial landscape. Other authors, while agreeing with the notion of divine energy, point to the fact that the artists always made reference to actual things which were emboldened by symbolic association. It has been argued that these "flowing" points could relate to the concept of running water, the wind, or the flight of insects (bees, termite *alates* and locusts) - things that artists knew in the natural world around them and given symbolic resonance.

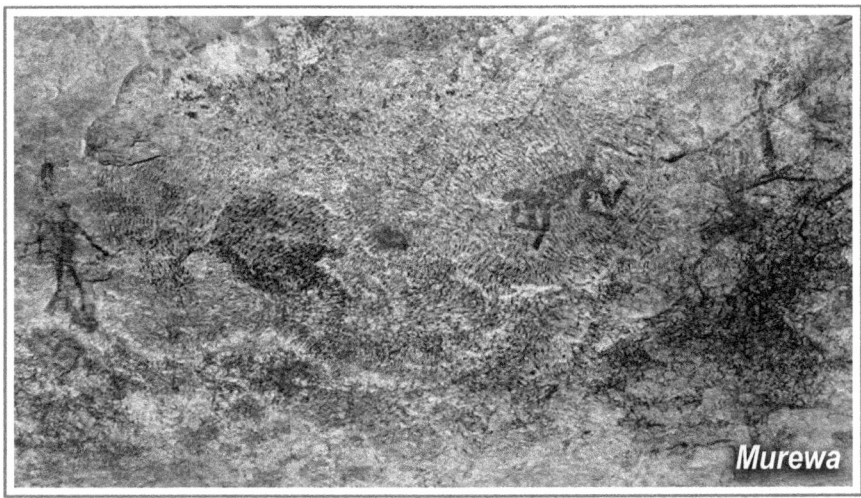
Murewa

Particularly notable features of Zimbabwean rock art are the strange partitioned, oval shapes found depicted in many caves. They are usually carefully painted, often outlined and covered in fine dots of other colours. Some are truly massive, a metre across or more. Others are smaller; but they are a consistent abstract theme found in our rock art.

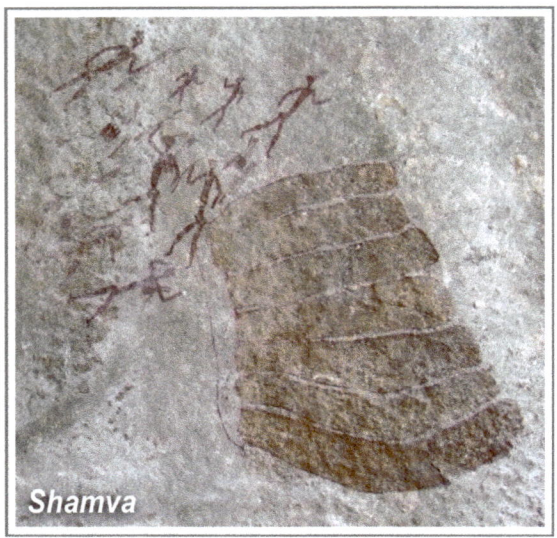

Named *formlings*, a meaningless word first coined by the German academic Leo Frobenius in the 1920s, these shapes have attracted many interpretations. Literalists have suggested that they are images of the granite landscapes, the boulder-strewn settings in which the art occurs, while one early author believed them to be impressionistic depictions of

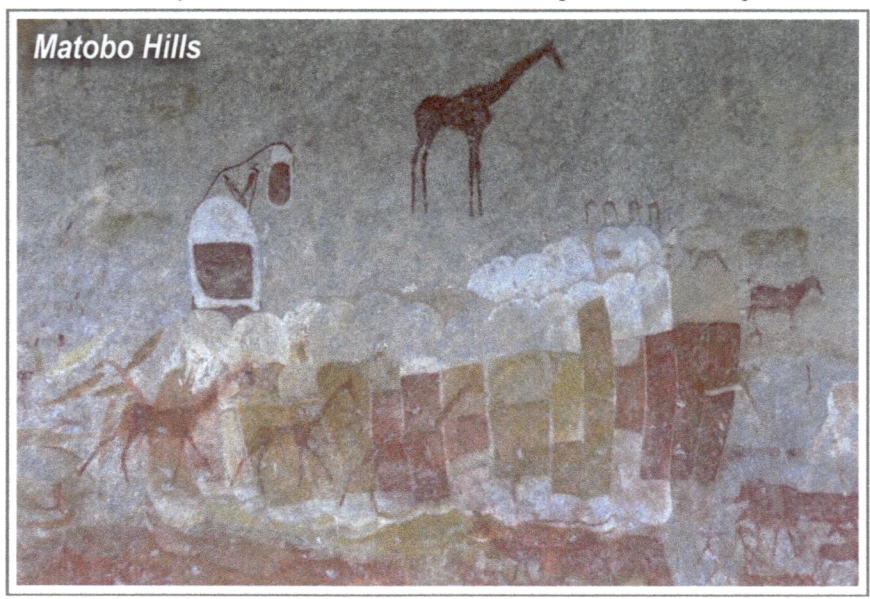

Victoria Falls! None of these explanations take into consideration Sān perception, nor do they account for the curious details of these shapes which include the multiple internal divisions, the dots and dashes, and crenellated margins.

Peter Garlake suggested that the *formlings* were entirely abstract, notions of some spiritual power, *n/om,* that the community would evoke during ceremonies. Others, while agreeing with the symbolic concept of divine power, suggest that the imagery is in fact based on a combination of real phenomena, with their added symbolic meanings. They have been described as the hives of the African honeybee which evokes associations

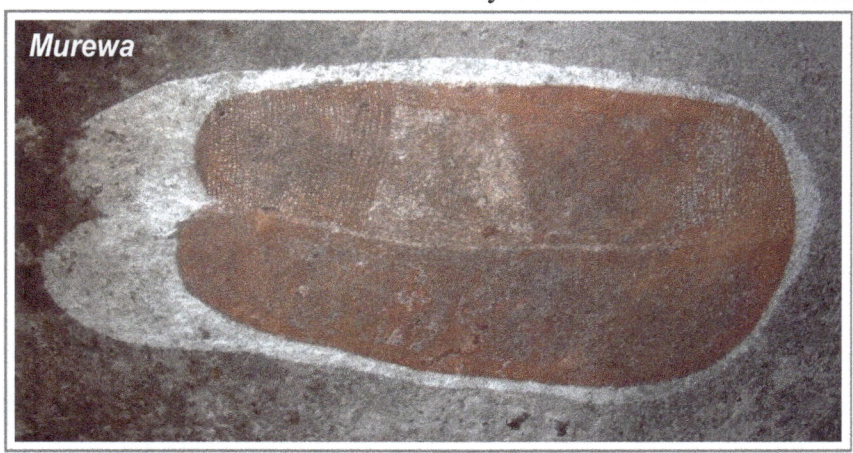

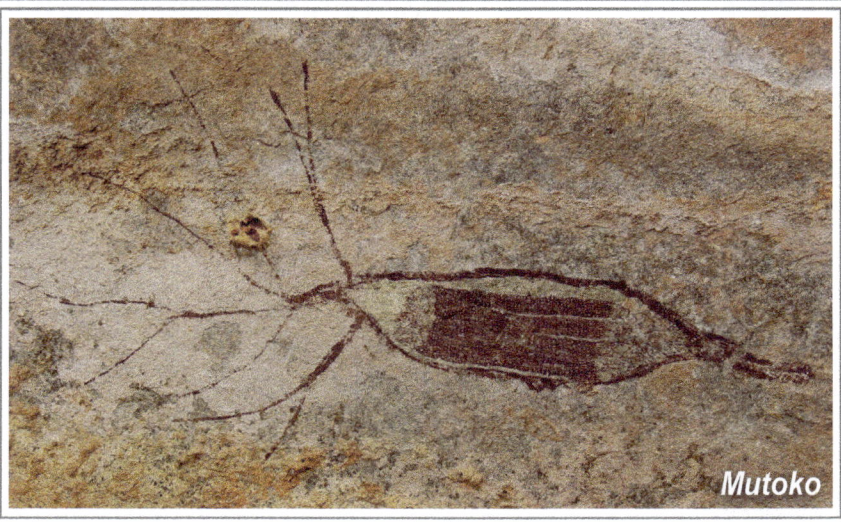

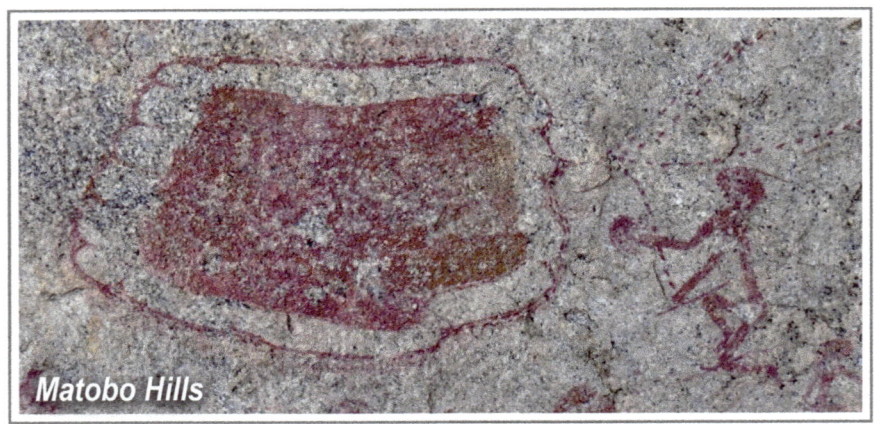

Matobo Hills

with honey, a rich sweetness not often available on the African veld. Others have said that they are wasp nests, which bring to mind the intense pain on being stung; something that may relate to the painful trance experiences of the shamans.

More recently, Siyakha Mguni has argued that they represent the central underground core of a termite colony and that this literal point of reference had deep symbolic meaning. The presence of the termite queen, bloated with fat; being the source of the *alates* (flying ants); and with its earthen towers, the termiterium was considered to be a metamorphic pathway linking the realm of the earth to that of the sky. The frequent association of many *formlings* with flows/swarms of dots, dashes and arrow marks, heighten the symbolic meaning. These are thought to represent the escaping *alates*, with the notion of *n/om* and/or trancing shaman.

It is probable that all of these associations are valid. The *formling* was polysemic, having multiple meanings. Often additional features were painted in association, further dramatising the *formling's* spiritual significance. In many cases, animals and humans appear to emerge from the ovals or were painted on top of them. In other instances, *formlings* were painted within or directly attached to the body of animals, human or plants. The combined symbolic composition is one of heightened power of all the component parts.

Then there are the strange circular patterns. We are not quite sure as to the precise meanings behind the meandering lines, painted spirals and large infilled blobs. Often these have attached human and animal

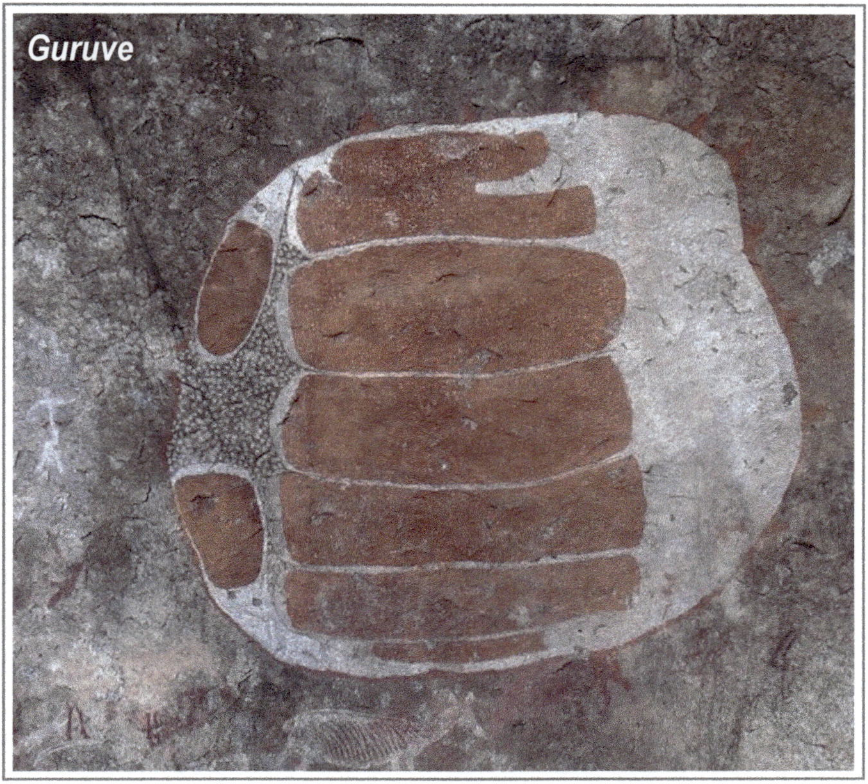

Guruve

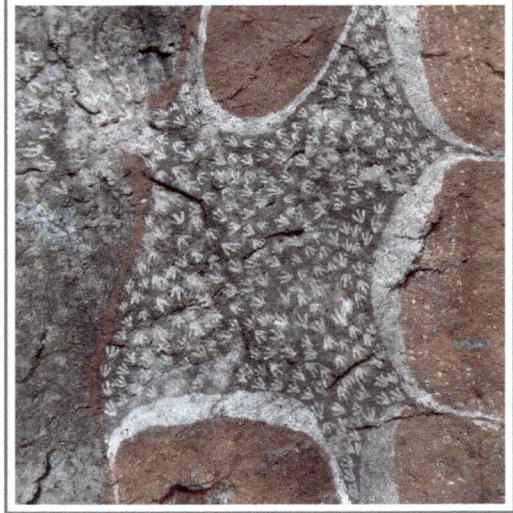

features, some originating from a human torso and ending in an animal head. They may be another expression of the same flow of power as represented by the lines of dots and dashes. They could be stylised representations of the flashing images, phosphenes, that shaman say they encounter on first entering an altered state of consciousness. They may be a portal to the spiritual

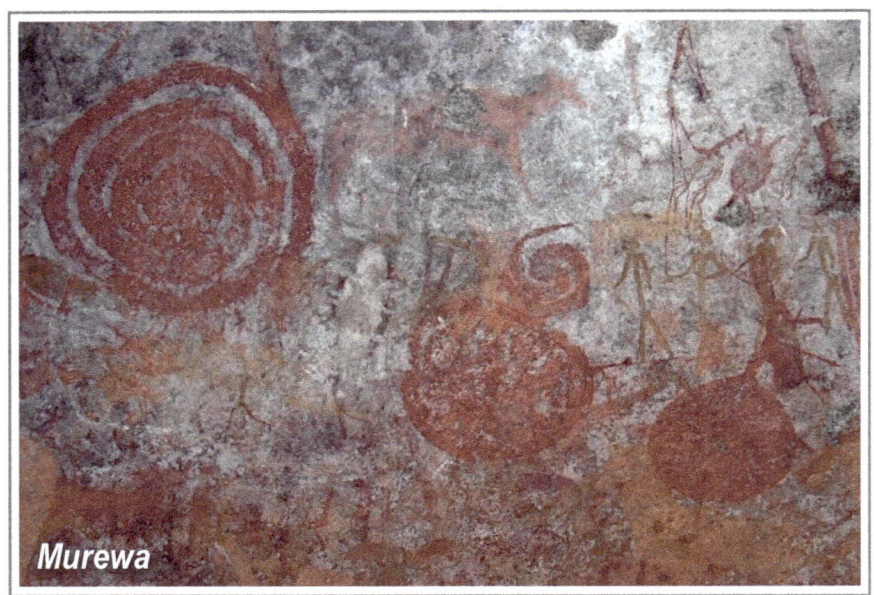
Murewa

realm, or the symbolically complicated pathway through life to "god's house"? Or they could symbolise the Sān cosmos, combining all in their daily lives and their spiritual realm? Any or all of these may apply, depending on the actual context.

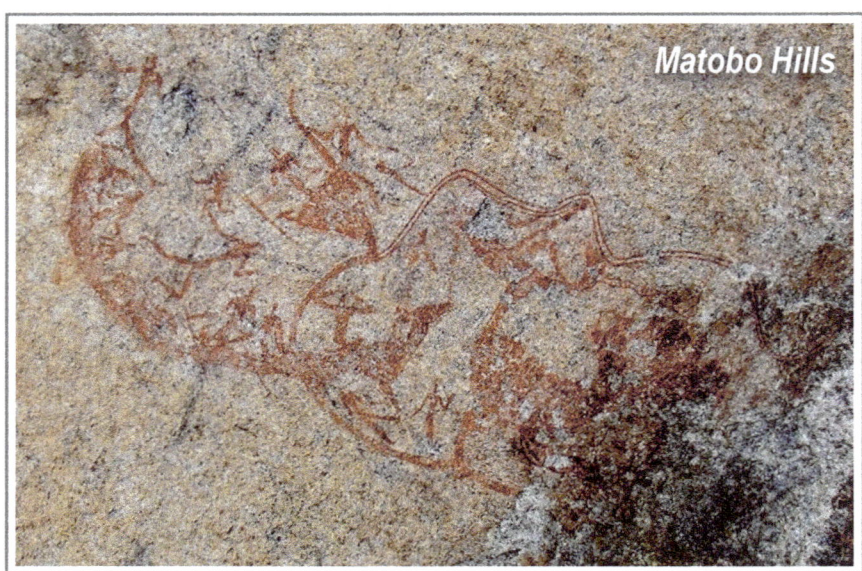
Matobo Hills

Zimbabwe's Exquisite Heritage

Undoubtedly we will have left many of our readers somewhat confused by the apparent ramblings of the text, but we need to understand that the art and its symbolic meanings are not straightforward. Our Sān rock art is no simple art of simple minds. Rather, it is deeply symbolic, consisting of select symbols that only make sense by understanding the worldview of the artists and their community. The art was a visual representation of their understanding of the cosmos and their interaction with it. Theirs is a different worldview to our own and no less complicated.

We never deny the artistic pleasure that can be derived from visiting the many painted sites scattered around the country, but we seek to go beyond mere optical self-gratification. So much more can be gained through understanding the very motives behind the art.

Underlying the selectivity of the symbols painted are human emotions and structures, made apparent through referral to literal features of the forager's worldly experience. These images should never be taken as literal, nor were meanings limited. Most of the painted symbols are polysemic, the context defining the meanings at any one time and place. We can never expect to understand fully, but can try to tease out some of their meanings. The art is as complex as the human mind and we are privileged to be able to enjoy it.

That said, Zimbabwe's rock art is facing a serious crisis, and could soon be completely lost to us. Yes, it has gradually faded over centuries because of exposure to the weather, but today the paintings are being rapidly destroyed as a result of human activity. Many of the caves are now used as places of worship. This is not a problem itself, but people are lighting huge fires in the caves and deliberately vandalising the art around them. At other sites, local school children have defaced it, scribbling their names and messages across the painted panels, silencing the voices of our past.

Should you be lucky enough to visit any of our painted sites, we ask that you respect the rights of local residents, rewarding them for sharing their treasures. Also, please don't touch the art, nor wet it with water to get a clearer view. Look at it, appreciate it for its complex meaning and the visual pleasure it provides. Listen to the ancient voices that speak from the rocks.

References

Some books which readers might find useful and which have moulded our own thoughts as to our rock art and approaches to understand it.

Cooke, C.K., Clark, J.D., & Goodall, E. 1959. *Prehistoric Rock Art of the Federation of Rhodesia & Nyasaland.* Salisbury: National Publications Trust.

Eastwood, E. & C. 2006. *Capturing the Spoor: an exploration of southern African rock art.* David Philip: Claremont.

Estes, R.D 1993. *The Safari Companion: a guide to watching African mammals.* Halfway House: Russell Friedman.

Garlake, P. 1987. *The Painted caves: an introduction to the prehistoric art of Zimbabwe.* Harare: Modus Publications.

Garlake, P. 1995. *The Hunter's Vision: the prehistoric rock art of Zimbabwe.* Harare: Zimbabwe Publishing House.

Jones, N. 1926. *The Stone Age in Rhodesia.* London: Oxford University Press.

Lewis-Williams, J.D. 1981. *Believing and Seeing: symbolic meanings in southern San rock paintings.* London: Academic Press.

Lewis-Williams, J.D. 1983. T*he Rock Art of Southern Africa.* Cambridge: Cambridge University Press.

Mguni, S. 2015. *Termites of the Gods: San cosmology in Southern African rock art.* Johannesburg: Wits University Press.

Nhamo, A. 2007. *Immortalizing the Past: reproductions of Zimbabwean rock art by Lionel Cripps.* Harare: Weaver Press.

Nhamo, A, Marufu, H., & Coulson, D. 2017. *The Rock Art of Mashonaland.* Nairobi: TARA (Trust for Africa Rock Art)

Parry, E. 2000. *Legacy on the Rocks: the prehistoric hunter-gatherers of the Matobo Hills, Zimbabwe.* Oxford: Oxbow.

Parry, E. 2002. *A Guide to the Rock Art of the Matobo Hills, Zimbabwe.* Bulawayo: Ama'Books.

Skotnes, P. (ed) 2007. *Claim to the Country: the archive of Wilhelm Bleek & Lucy Lloyd.* Johannesburg: Jacana Press..

Tredgold, R. 1956. *The Matopos.* Lusaka: Federal Department of Printing.

Vinnicombe, P. 1976. *People of the Eland.* Pietermaritzburg: University of Natal Press.

Walker, N. 1986. *The Painted Hills: rock art of the Matopos.* Gweru: Mambo Press.

There are many more publications and articles on the rock art of Zimbabwe and Southern Africa in general. The reader is advised to seek these out and to read widely.

www.ingramcontent.com/pod-product-compliance
Lightning Source LLC
Chambersburg PA
CBHW040521220526
45473CB00013B/2945

Overtime List

Department	First Name	Last Name	Emp. ID	Dia 1	Dia 2	Dia 3	Dia 4	Dia 5	Dia 6	Dia 7
Cutters										
Cutters										
Cutters										
Cutters										
Cutters										
Cutters										
Cutters										
Cutters										
Cutters										
Cutters										
Cutters										
Cutters										
Cutters										
Cutters										
Cutters										
Scanners										
Scanners										
Scanners										
Scanners										
Scanners										
Scanners										
Scanners										
Scanners										
Scanners										
Scanners										
Scanners										
Scanners										
Scanners										
Scanners										
Receiving										
Receiving										
Receiving										
Receiving										
Receiving										
Receiving										
Receiving										
Receiving										
Receiving										
Receiving										
Receiving										
Receiving										
Receiving										
Receiving										
Support										
Support										
Support										
Support										
Support										